# CHRISTIANITY:
# THE WITNESS OF HISTORY

# CHRISTIANITY:
# THE WITNESS OF HISTORY

A LAWYER'S APPROACH

J. N. D. ANDERSON, O.B.E., LL.D.

*Professor of Oriental Laws, and Director of the*
*Institute of Advanced Legal Studies in the University of London*

TYNDALE PRESS
39 BEDFORD SQUARE, LONDON WC1

© THE TYNDALE PRESS

*First Edition October 1969*

STANDARD BOOK NUMBER 85111 305 2

This book is based on a series of lectures given in October 1969 at Trent University, Ontario, Canada.

Biblical quotations, unless otherwise indicated, are from the Revised Standard Version of the Bible, copyrighted in 1946 and 1952 by the Division of Christian Education, National Council of the Churches of Christ in the USA.

*Printed and bound in Great Britain by*
*Billing & Sons Limited, Guildford and London*

# CONTENTS

# PREFACE

'Is it relevant?' is one of the first questions asked about anything today. This is fair enough; and it should serve as a salutary reminder, not only to the academic in his proverbial ivory tower but also to the pious purveyor of traditional doctrines, that he must always ask himself whether his research on the one hand, or his return to well-worn paths on the other, is of any practical value.

Why, then, should this book concern itself primarily with the first rather than the twentieth century? Are the events of nearly two thousand years ago really so vitally important today? Should not Christianity be judged by the moral impact of its ethical teaching on the problems which face us now? Or should it be judged, perhaps, by the comfort and inspiration it affords to those who are hard put to it to sustain, let alone rise above, the stresses, strains and sorrows of the 'secular city' – or of any other manifestation of contemporary life? In a word, should it not be evaluated by existential, rather than historical, criteria?

In this context it is important to remember that Christianity has always been accompanied by existential phenomena. The man born blind, of whom we read in John's Gospel, refused to indulge, in his confrontation with the Pharisees, in theological arguments, but stubbornly reiterated that there was one thing he knew for certain – that, whereas he had been blind, now he could see. And Saul of Tarsus, on the road to Damascus, underwent a vivid existential experience.

But existential experience is not enough by itself. There must be an adequate basis for the alleged experience if it is to be meaningful to others; and there must be some way by which the facts or ideas behind it can be tested and examined.

A Muslim Professor in Cairo, a well-known authority on Islamic history, once remarked to me that religion, in his view, was not so much a matter of science as of art. When I asked what he meant by this, he explained that in a scientific monograph the strict accuracy of all the relevant facts was of fundamental importance, while in a poem the basic question was not whether every detail would stand up to scientific analysis, but rather the aesthetic impact of the composition as a whole. Similarly, in matters of religion, the criterion was not whether the facts on which Christianity, Islam, or any other religion was said to rest would stand up to historical investigation, but whether the religion concerned made those who followed it happier in themselves and more helpful to others.

I replied – somewhat flippantly, I fear – that when I was a boy at school we played a football match against what was then called a lunatic asylum. (I vividly remember being locked in while we changed our clothes, so that we should not get mixed up with the other lunatics!) And we were told that one of the patients in that institution firmly believed that he was a poached egg, and went about every day asking for a piece of toast to sit on. If he was given this, he at once became contented and amenable, while if it was withheld he remained unhappy and fractious. But I could hardly believe that my Muslim friend would regard that as an adequate religion!

This was, no doubt, an extreme and somewhat absurd illustration. But it is obvious that other beliefs based on existential criteria, entertained by much more normal and rational people, may equally prove to be ill-founded. They may, indeed, sustain a man for as long as he believes them; but his disappointment and disillusionment when he comes to realize they are false will be in direct proportion to the fervour of his former conviction. And if a man is sustained through life by a conviction which concerns not only time but eternity, only to find at the end that it was an illusion and a mockery, that would be stark tragedy.

C. S. Lewis tells a story, in *Mere Christianity*,[1] of an officer

[1] Fontana, 1955, pp. 130f.

in the RAF who, after listening to a talk on Christianity, burst out with the protest: 'I've no use for all that stuff. But, mind you, I'm a religious man too. I know there's a God. I've felt Him: out alone in the desert at night: the tremendous mystery. And that's just why I don't believe all your neat little dogmas and formulas about Him. To anyone who's met the real thing they all seem so petty and pedantic and unreal!' And Lewis remarks that, in a sense, he quite agreed. The man may well have had a real experience of some sort in the desert, and when he turned from that experience to a talk on what Christians believe he may have felt that he was turning from reality to something less real. 'In the same way,' Lewis writes, 'if a man has once looked at the Atlantic from the beach, and then goes and looks at a map of the Atlantic, he also will be turning from something real to something less real: turning from real waves to a bit of coloured paper. But here comes the point. The map is admittedly only coloured paper, but there are two things you have to remember about it. In the first place, it is based on what hundreds and thousands of people have found out by sailing the real Atlantic. In that way it has behind it masses of experience just as real as the one you could have from the beach; only, while yours would be a single isolated glimpse, the map fits all those different experiences together. In the second place, if you want to go anywhere, the map is absolutely necessary. As long as you are content with walks on the beach, your own glimpses are far more fun than looking at a map. But the map is going to be more use than walks on the beach if you want to get to America.'

It seems obvious, then, that the existential experiences of any one individual can be regarded as having no more than a subjective value for himself alone unless they can be tested and compared with those of others. But it is often asserted today that such experiences are, in their very nature, incommunicable. Francis Schaeffer writes that Karl Jaspers, for example, lays a great deal of emphasis on the need to wait for a non-rational 'final experience' which would give meaning to life. People who follow Jaspers have come to Schaeffer and said 'I have had a final experience', but they never expect him to ask them what it was. If he did, it would prove that he was not among the initiated. The very fact that it was an *existential* experience meant that it could not be communicated. Such people sometimes recognize, it seems, that Schaeffer himself has had a 'final experience' and comment on this fact; but when he tells them that his experience can be verbalized and rationally discussed, they reply that this is impossible, and that he is trying to do something that cannot be done.[2]

But it is basic to the Christian experience that it can not only be expressed in words – however inadequately – and compared with that of others, but that it is intimately connected with the Christ who lived and died nearly two thousand years ago. Christians, of course, believe that he rose again from the grave and is a living Saviour with whom they can have an existential encounter today. But unless the one with whom they have this encounter is the same Christ about whom the Gospels speak, the encounter they claim to have had is not authentically Christian. It is fatally easy for the human mind to construct a 'Jesus' of its own imagining.

This is why it is essential to go back to the first century and consider the phenomena presented by the New Testament, as we shall attempt to do in this book. First, by way of prolegomenon, we shall examine the historical basis on which the whole Christian revelation rests and ask ourselves whether it is convincing. Next, we shall concentrate on the person of Christ as depicted in the Gospels and try to make up our minds, on the evidence, what conclusion we must reach about him. Then we shall turn our attention to his death on a Roman gibbet and consider whether this was in fact inevitable and how it should be understood. Finally, we shall weigh the evidence for the empty tomb and risen Lord of the New Testament testimony and try to decide whether this rests on fact or fancy, on historical event or mythological reconstruction.

Professor C. F. D. Moule, in *The Phenomenon of the New Testament*,[3] quotes D. E. Jenkins' remark that 'Christianity is based on indisputable facts . . . I do not say that Christianity is the indisputable interpretation of these facts' and then proceeds: 'It is precisely some of these indisputable facts that I here present, asking whether the Christian interpretation,

[2] *The God Who is There* (Hodder and Stoughton, 1968), pp. 22, 23.
[3] SCM Press, 1967, p. 3.

though I agree that it is not indisputable, is not by far the most plausible – almost (I would venture to think) the inescapable – interpretation.'

It is true, as Moule observes, that 'rational conviction, even when it can be had, is very different from commitment. . . . Commitment to Christ is a matter for the entire person, not for his mind alone; and intellectual conviction (if, indeed, it can be had at all without the whole person being involved) is not the whole business. But the whole business, precisely because it concerns the whole person, can never be achieved in defiance of the intellect. Reason, though not the whole, is part of personal response.'[4] Indeed, intellectual conviction constitutes, in a very real sense, the essential basis for the self-commitment of any rational and moral being, made in the 'image' of his creator.

But where is such intellectual conviction to be found? The essence of the sense of frustration and despair which seems to characterize contemporary thought is the denial that basic questions about God, man and human destiny can ever receive an authoritative answer. It is to such that the Jesus of the New Testament furnishes what Dr Carnegie Simpson terms 'the most patent and accessible of data'. What are these data? Not metaphysical ideas or unverifiable sentiments, but concerned with a historical person, who constitutes 'a fact as available as any other fact'. And he pertinently asks how many of those who assume an agnostic attitude to religion have honestly brought their minds and hearts and consciences face to face with the fact of Christ, and candidly considered if it means anything to them for religion. 'It is impossible to say that no one has the right to be an agnostic. But no one has the right to be an agnostic till he has thus dealt with the question,' and faced this fact with an open mind. After that, he may be an agnostic – if he can.[5]

[4] *Ibid.*, pp. 5, 6.
[5] *The Fact of Christ* (James Clarke, 1952 edition), pp. 8, 9.

# 1 THE HISTORICAL BASIS:
## IS IT CONVINCING?

We live in an age of comparative studies. This is partly a reaction against the narrow specialization to which the vast output of contemporary scholarship condemns most of us in our reading and research, but it also represents a recognition of the light which other systems of law, political theory or religion can throw on our own. In the sphere of religion this impulse has been inspired by a new spirit of sympathy and understanding, which is greatly to be welcomed. But it has resulted, all too often, in an unprecedented attitude of personal detachment, which certainly makes an objective evaluation of data somewhat easier, but may well make any first-hand experience of faith correspondingly more difficult.

Religions can, of course, be compared at a number of different levels. We can make a comparative study of the philosophy which lies behind them, or the theological teaching which is peculiar to each. We can compare their ethical demands, their liturgical legacy, their historical development, their missionary enthusiasm or their impact on the thought and conduct of their adherents. All these different approaches are, moreover, eminently relevant to a comparative study of Christianity as one among the world's great religions. But it seems to me inescapable that anyone who chanced to read the pages of the New Testament for the first time would come away with one overwhelming impression – that here is a faith firmly rooted in certain allegedly historical events, a faith which would be false and misleading if those events had not actually taken place, but which, if they did take place, is unique in its relevance and exclusive in its demands on our allegiance. For these events did not merely set a 'process in

motion and then themselves sink back into the past. To the
unique historical origin of Christianity is ascribed permanent,
authoritative, absolute significance: what happened once
is said to have happened once for all and therefore to have
continuous efficacy.'[1]

But this assessment of the Christian faith has been challenged from two different angles. First, there are many today
from inside the tradition of Christendom who would question,
in varying degrees, the historical basis on which the message
of the New Testament is founded. Secondly, there are others,
both from inside and outside that tradition, who would deny
that Christianity, whatever its basis in history, can be regarded
as unique in its authority or final in its claims.

Those who question the historical events which the New
Testament consistently postulates as the genesis, foundation
and content of the Christian message do not, of course, doubt
the historical phenomenon of the eruption of the Christian
faith on the Graeco-Roman world, the joy and spontaneity of
the early Christians, or even – in the vast majority of cases –
the fact that the Jesus to whom they attributed their faith
was no figment of their imagination. It is true that a few isolated individuals have tried to dismiss the unique figure
which dominates the New Testament as a beautiful myth;
and this attitude, as adopted by Karl Marx, has become
widespread in Communist thinking. But it has been justly
remarked that the arguments put forward to support this
theory 'have again and again been answered and annihilated
by first-rank scholars'.[2] More recently, John Allegro has gone
back to this hypothesis with the suggestion that the Christ
of the Gospels was a mere reflection or reconstruction of the
'Teacher of Righteousness' who inspired the community of
the Dead Sea Scrolls.[3] But Allegro's wild theorizing about the

---

[1] Heinz Zahrnt, *The Historical Jesus* (Collins, 1963), p. 27.
[2] Roderic Dunkerley, *Beyond the Gospels* (Penguin Books, 1957), p. 12.
[3] Allegro indicated (in a lecture at Richmond on 29 March 1968) that he
had now come to see that the Teacher of Righteousness could not bear the
burden of explaining away Christianity. But he still, apparently, permitted
himself asides such as, 'if we suppose for a fleeting moment that John the
Baptist existed . . . If Jesus existed . . .' (see *The Christian and Christianity
Today*, 12 April 1968, p. 28). Yet in his scholarly work *Search in the Desert*
(W. H. Allen, 1965), p. 173, he has acknowledged that '. . . the real issues

relationship between Christianity and the community of the Scrolls has been refuted and repudiated by a galaxy of experts,[4] and it is, I think, true to say that the vast majority of both scholars and laymen would agree with Sir James Frazer that 'The doubts which have been cast on the historical reality of Jesus are, in my judgement, unworthy of serious attention'.[5] More recently, Otto Betz has committed himself to the statement that, in recent years, 'no serious scholar has ventured to postulate the non-historicity of Jesus.'[6]

No, it is not the historical reality of Jesus himself which is seriously in doubt today – although to this we must subsequently return – but rather the historicity of what is said about him in the New Testament and the relevance or irrelevance of such historicity. The teaching of the apostolic church about the person and work of Jesus can, of course, scarcely be called in question, for to this the New Testament bears unequivocal witness. The point at issue is how far this teaching can be explained in terms of a mythology which reflects and symbolizes the subjective belief and experience of the apostles and their followers rather than objective, historical facts on which that belief and experience were founded. It is even suggested that historical factuality is irrelevant in this context except for the most minimal anchoring in history of the sum-

---

have been overlaid too often by special pleading in attempts to prove the falsity or truth of Christianity on the basis of the new evidence. The Scrolls do neither. The light they have brought has been upon the immediate background of Christianity, in particular, the kind of Judaism from which Christianity probably evolved.'

[4] Cf. the letter published in The Times on 21 December 1965 over the signatures of G. R. Driver, Emeritus Professor of Semitic Philology, Oxford University; H. H. Rowley, Emeritus Professor of Hebrew, Manchester University; Peter R. Ackroyd, Professor of Old Testament Studies, London University; Matthew Black, Professor of Biblical Criticism, St Andrew's University; J. B. Segal, Professor of Semitic Languages, London University; D. Winton Thomas, Regius Professor of Hebrew, Cambridge University; Edward Ullendorff, Professor of Ethiopian Studies, London University; D. J. Wiseman, Professor of Assyriology, London University. 'Nothing that appears in the Scrolls hitherto discovered throws any doubt on the originality of Christianity . . . nor is there any hint that the Rightful Teacher may have been regarded as in any sense divine.'

[5] The Golden Bough (Macmillan, 1913), Vol. 9, p. 412n.

[6] What do we know about Jesus? (SCM Press, 1968), p. 9.

mons to decision, and that all that matters is that men and
women can still come to the same basic experience which the
early church expressed in these mythological terms.

But this seems strangely alien to the attitude of the New
Testament writers themselves. That attitude can, I think,
best be summarized in Paul's categorical assertion that 'if
Christ was not raised then neither our preaching nor your
faith has any meaning at all. Further it would mean that we
are lying in our witness for God, for we have given our solemn
testimony that he did raise up Christ.'[7] Nor was this testimony
confined to any vague or general affirmation that the crucified
Christ had been exalted and glorified; it included explicit
reference to several of the resurrection appearances, and an
implicit reference to the empty tomb.[8] And the significance of
this passage lies not only in the fact that it is so emphatic
and clear-cut, but that it comes in an epistle whose Pauline
authorship and very early date are accepted by every reput-
able scholar.[9] But the same fundamental attitude underlies
the whole New Testament: the Gospels profess to record the
historical events; the Acts of the Apostles to summarize the
witness of both Peter and Paul, shared by the other apostles,
first to the objective reality of these events and then to their
subjective significance; the Epistles to elaborate the meaning
of these events in the life of the church and its members; and
the book of Revelation to deal with these same events in
terms of their eternal and transcendental significance.

That this is the attitude of the New Testament writers
seems to me inescapable. But can we accept the claim that their
faith had any adequate historical foundation? Is this credible
in the twentieth century? What evidence can be adduced in
its support?

Before we turn to consider the evidence we should, I think,
pause to observe that the answer to this question will go a very
long way towards providing the answer to our second major
question about the Christian faith: whether it can justly be
regarded as unique in its authority and final in its claims. For
an examination of its historical origins will necessarily lead
us to consider, in subsequent chapters, the evidence for three

[7] 1 Cor. 15:14, 15, J. B. Phillips' translation.
[8] See chapter 4, pp. 84f.                    [9] See below, pp. 27f.

crucial tenets of Christian belief: first, that Jesus Christ was not merely a very good man who could point men to God somewhat more effectively than any other human teacher, but was God incarnate; secondly, that the death he died cannot be explained simply as a tragedy of martyrdom or a supreme example of unselfishness, but was God's own remedy for human sin; and, thirdly, that he rose again on the third day, and that this resurrection must, in the light of all he had previously taught, be regarded as a clear authentication both of the reality of his deity and the efficacy of his atoning death.

No-one in their senses would deny for a moment that the other world religions include much that is true and helpful, or that Christians can learn a great deal from the earnestness and devotion of their followers. I nthe Christian view, all that is true ultimately comes from God, mediated through Christ himself as the eternal 'Word' of the Father. But the other world religions also comprise much that is false and misleading – pre-eminently in the fact that they inevitably deny, at least by implication, God's unique revelation of himself in the incarnation, the atonement and the resurrection. So the Christian must inevitably ask: If God could have *adequately* revealed himself in any other way, would he have gone to the incredible length of the manger of Bethlehem and all that was involved in the incarnation? That, surely, would not make sense. Again, if God could have found any other solution to the problem of human sin, would he have gone all the way, in the person of his Son, to the crucifixion? That, too, would not make sense.

Precisely the same questions may be used to demonstrate that the Christian faith is not only unique but final. For if God has so revealed himself, what repetition or addition can be required or envisaged? If God has so reconciled men to himself, what further remedy for sin can either God or man desire? Inevitably, therefore, the Christian faith claims for itself, in the words of Stephen Neill, that it is the 'only form of faith for men', and by its own claim to truth it inescapably 'casts the shadow of falsehood, or at least of imperfect truth, on every other system'. Here there is a sharply contrasted thesis and antithesis, and no synthesis or syncretism is possible. 'This Christian claim', he continues, 'is naturally offensive to the adherents of every other religious system. It is almost as offensive to modern man, brought up in the atmosphere of relativism, in which tolerance is regarded almost as the highest of the virtues. But we must not suppose that this claim to universal validity is something that can quietly be removed from the Gospel without changing it into something entirely different from what it is. The mission of Jesus was limited to the Jews and did not look immediately beyond them; but his life, his method and his message do not make sense, unless they are interpreted in the light of his own conviction that he was in fact the final and decisive word of God to men. . . . For the human sickness there is one specific remedy, and this is it. There is no other.'[1]

This is a stupendous assertion. Is it credible? And what standing has a lawyer, anyway, in such a study? Surely this should be left to the historian and the theologian, as those professionally qualified to evaluate the historical evidence and then assess its significance? But it may be suggested in reply that in this case a significant part of the historical evidence comes from a consideration of facts and circumstances which must, from their very nature, be weighed and examined in a way which is not unfamiliar to the lawyer. He will necessarily be dependent on others for an evaluation of the documentary evidence as such; but he has, perhaps, a certain competence of his own in deciding what that evidence seems to establish, and must claim the right to assess the conclusions of the experts by his own criteria.

Now for all the details of the origins of Christianity we are dependent on the New Testament, to which we must soon turn our attention. But is there no documentary evidence whatever from non-Christian sources? Can no pagan or Jewish writers be cited in support?

The answer is that such evidence does exist, but that it is somewhat meagre. The earliest reference which has come down to us from any Roman document is in a letter written by the younger Pliny to the Emperor Trajan from Bithynia in about AD 110, in which he gives a picture of the early Christian community gathering in the early morning, once a week, to 'sing a hymn to Christ as to a god' and again, on

[1] *Christian Faith and Other Faiths* (Oxford University Press, 1961), pp. 16, 17.

the evening of the same day, to partake of a common meal; they refused to worship the imperial statue or the images of the gods, they lived exemplary lives, and some of them were willing to face death rather than deny their faith. There is also a terse reference in Tacitus, dated some five years later, to 'Christ, who was executed in the reign of Tiberius by the procurator Pontius Pilate';[2] and it is scarcely fanciful to suggest that when he adds that 'A most mischievous super- stition, thus checked for the moment, again broke out' he is bearing indirect and unconscious testimony to the conviction of the early church that the Christ who had been crucified had risen from the grave. There is also a probable reference to Christ in Suetonius, dated about AD 120, where he tells us that Claudius expelled the Jews from Rome because they were constantly making disturbances at the instigation of 'Chrestus' – for it seems that Suetonius mistook the split in the Jewish community in Rome which resulted from the Christian pro- clamation that Christ was still alive for a factional strife in which he was himself the leader of one of the parties.[3]

In addition, there is a certain amount of secondary evidence, in the form of quotations from earlier pagan writers preserved in the books of third-century Christian authors. Origen, for example, states that Phlegon (a freedman of the Emperor Hadrian who was born about AD 80) mentioned that the founder of Christianity had made certain predictions which had proved true. Again, Julius Africanus informs us that 'Thallus, in the third book of his history' attributed the darkness at the crucifixion of Christ to an eclipse of the sun; and there is good reason to believe that this Thallus was a Samaritan historian who wrote about the middle of the first century.[4] If this identification is correct, then from this and other evidence it seems clear that the circumstances surround- ing the origin of Christianity were being discussed by non- Christians at a very early date. It is also distinctly possible that an inscription found in Nazareth in which the Emperor – either Claudius or even Tiberius – expresses his displeasure at reports he has heard of the removal of dead bodies from

[2] *Annals* xi. 44.
[3] *Life of Claudius*; *cf.* R. Dunkerley, *Beyond the Gospels*, pp. 25f.
[4] See Dunkerley, pp. 27ff.

their graves, and even threatens the death penalty for such action, represents an echo of the report which must surely have reached Rome about the crucifixion of one accused of political pretensions whose body had subsequently disappeared from the tomb.[5] But however that may be, the pagan evidence for the historicity of Jesus and his crucifixion under Pontius Pilate is such that it would be accepted without question in relation to anyone else.

When we turn to Jewish sources the testimony of Josephus in his *Jewish War*, written between AD 70 and 75, is somewhat controversial. In the Greek version there are no references to Christ whatever, but there are some eight references in the Slavonic (or old Russian) version. These are often discounted, but it is at least possible that this version was based on a Greek translation of an earlier Aramaic draft which Josephus is known to have made. Be that as it may, his *Jewish Antiquities*, of some twenty years later, includes references to John the Baptist, to James 'the brother of Jesus, who was called Christ', and to Jesus himself in a longer passage which has been the subject of much controversy. Its essence reads as follows: 'And there arose about this time Jesus, a wise man, if indeed he should be called a man. For he was a doer of marvellous deeds, a teacher of men. . . . This man was the Christ. And when Pilate had condemned him to the cross at the instigation of our own leaders, those who had loved him from the first did not cease. For he appeared to them on the third day alive again . . . And even now the tribe of Christians named after him is not extinct.'[6]

This has often been dismissed as a Christian interpolation, on the grounds that it goes considerably further than would be likely from a non-Christian. But it would be equally plausible to argue that it does not go quite so far as a Christian interpolation might be expected to go. Some of its phrases, of course, may well have been written in a vein of sarcasm, and it has even been described as a 'masterpiece of non-committal statement'. But whether or not it has been subjected to any Christian 'editing', it is difficult completely to ignore it, since it has as good manuscript evidence as anything in Josephus.

[5] *Cf.* E. M. Blaiklock, *Layman's Answer* (Hodder and Stoughton, 1968), pp. 28f.   [6] *Ant.* xviii. 3.3.

There are also a number of relevant references in the *Mishna*, or oral law (*i.e.* 'tradition of the elders', compiled between 100 BC and AD 200) and in the *Gemara* (*i.e.* comments of the Rabbis, compiled between AD 200 and 500). One of these begins, 'On the eve of the Passover they hanged Yeshu of Nazareth.' Another reads, 'Rabbi Shimeon ben Azzai said . . . "such-an-one is a bastard of an adulteress" ', and a third, 'Rabbi Eliezer said "Balaam looked forth and saw that there was a man, born of a woman, who should rise up and seek to make himself God, and to cause the whole world to go astray . . . and he will deceive and say that he departeth and cometh again at the end" .'

These and other passages are accepted as references to Jesus by J. Klausner, a Jewish scholar, in his study *Jesus of Nazareth*.[7] Naturally enough, they are of a hostile nature; but they are of considerable value as providing independent evidence which can scarcely be called in question not only to the historicity of Christ but to stories which were current about the unusual circumstances of his birth (with a scurrilous interpretation, which was, perhaps, only to be expected), his divine claims, his crucifixion and his reputed resurrection.

A brief reference must also be made to the testimony of archaeology. One of the most intriguing problems is posed by the Sator-Rotas acrostic, which takes the form of a complete word square (and perfect palindrome) and was regarded for centuries as having almost magical powers. Its surface meaning – something to the effect that 'the sower holds the wheels of the plough with care' – could not possibly account for its widespread use in the early church. A persuasive conjecture about its secret meaning is that its letters, if arranged in the form of a cross, represent a twice-repeated 'Pater Noster' plus an additional A and O (standing for Alpha and Omega, or Jesus as the beginning and the end, the origin and the goal of all creation). As Dunkerley says, 'We may surmise that the original author in the first place arranged the two sacred words Pater Noster in the form of a cross . . . as a kind of holy remembrancer or aid to devotion. Then, at a time of persecution – perhaps the Neronian – he framed the square to contain yet conceal the beloved teaching. Lacking four

[7] George Allen and Unwin, 1925, pp. 27, 34f.

letters, however, for a five-word square, he very skilfully chose the other two sacred letters, A and O . . . and repeated them twice. The very fact . . . of the difficulty . . . of getting an exact and satisfactory interpretation of the sentence may itself point in this direction – he did his best within the limits of the available letters, but the result was not entirely perfect.'[8]

Read differently – and without any rearrangement whatever – the same acrostic can be seen as again including the sign of the cross formed by the repetition, vertically and horizontally, of the word 'Tenet' (he holds) – attention being called to this concealed cross by the T (an accepted symbol of the cross in the primitive church[9]) with which both the vertical and horizontal bars begin and end. This would represent a vivid reminder not only of the centrality of the cross, with its message of forgiveness, but of the keeping power of the risen Lord which could, and did, sustain those going through the agonies of martyrdom. And this acrostic was in use very early indeed, since it has been found even in the ruins of Pompeii, destroyed in AD 79.[1]

Another very common Christian symbol, from the earliest days, was the sign of a fish. The significance of this was that the five letters in the Greek word for fish (*ichthys*) stand for 'Jesus Christ, Son of God, Saviour' – which represents a brief, but remarkably comprehensive, Christian creed. But none of this, as it seems to me, adds very much to what we already know from the pages of the New Testament. What these archaeological discoveries prove is that there is testimony, even outside the New Testament, to what Christians believed at an exceedingly early date. And archaeological excavations have again and again vindicated the historical accuracy of the New Testament documents – *e.g.* the Acts of the Apostles – in regard to details which had previously been called in question, or even ridiculed, by critics.

When we turn to the New Testament we find an abundance of detail which is in marked contrast to the paucity of non-Christian material. Nor is this in any way surprising. On the contrary, it is precisely what we might expect. Neither Josephus nor Tacitus lived in Palestine at the time when Jesus

[8] R. Dunkerley, *Beyond the Gospels*, p. 61; see also pp. 58–62.
[9] *Cf. Epistle of Barnabas* ix. 8.          [1] *Cf.* Dunkerley, p. 58.

of Nazareth lived and taught, or when he died on a Roman
gibbet; and nothing has come down to us written by any Jew,
Roman or Greek who had any first-hand evidence to record.
Roman historians and men of letters were scarcely likely to
have taken much interest in 'an obscure peasant teacher in an
unimportant frontier province', so it would not have been
surprising if the humble birth of Christianity had gone completely unnoticed in such circles; and it has been remarked
that Josephus wrote with the intention of re-establishing
Judaism with Roman society in general and the imperial
house in particular, so he naturally kept to a minimum any
material which would irritate Roman readers.[2] It is clear from
the Gospels that Jesus himself led no rebellion and made no
such dramatic gesture in defiance of authority as would
attract the attention of a Roman historian.[3] Instead, he
confided the 'good news' of who he was, what he had done and
what he had taught to a little band of chosen eyewitnesses,
feeble as they were, and to the work which the divine Spirit
was to do in them and through them.

We must, therefore, take as our major starting-point the
faith and teaching of the primitive church as we find it
throughout the New Testament, for about this, at least, there
can be no doubt whatever. The early Christians clearly
believed – and we shall discuss these phrases later – that
Jesus of Nazareth was the Son of God, the very agent of
creation, who had been made man, had proclaimed the kingdom of God, wrought miracles, gone about doing good, and
had finally died on the cross for the sins of mankind. But on the
third day he rose again, showed himself alive to his disciples
by 'many infallible proofs' and ascended into heaven, with
the promise that one day he would return to usher in a new
heaven and new earth, with the resurrection of the dead and
the final judgment.[4] So they proceeded to apply to him all
manner of honorific titles. They called him Messiah, Son of
Man, Son of David, Son of God, Redeemer, Saviour, Lord,

[2] Cf. Michael Green, *Runaway World* (Inter-Varsity Press, 1968), which
gives a most readable summary of the historical evidence.
[3] *Pace* S. G. F. Brandon, *The Trial of Jesus of Nazareth* (Batsford, 1968),
pp. 67, 84, 102, 104, 146–150, *etc.*
[4] *Cf.* Heinz Zahrnt, *The Historical Jesus*, pp. 44ff.

Logos, God.[5] And it is noteworthy that the quotation by Paul in 1 Corinthians 16:22 of the Aramaic prayer *Maranatha* ('Our Lord, come') shows that the title 'Lord' goes back to a Palestinian, rather than Greek, origin.[6]

But the question necessarily arises as to whether this teaching about the exalted Christ has any vital connection with the historical Jesus on whom it was professedly based. For many years now it has been fashionable to postulate a veritable gulf between the 'Lord of faith' and the 'Jesus of history'.[7] At first the emphasis was firmly placed on an attempt to get behind 'Pauline Christianity' and to rediscover the Jesus who walked and talked beside the Sea of Galilee. The attitude of mind of the scholars of what may be termed the era of Liberal Protestantism was that the Jesus of history meant something very different from the Jesus preached by the church. 'It meant Jesus as we can know him when we have dismantled the Church's preaching about him, and have penetrated behind it to find the real, actual, historical Jesus, Jesus as he historically was, Jesus the human historical personality, unsullied by dogma and undistorted by later ecclesiastical interpretation, be it Pauline or Johannine, Jewish or Greek. . . . The Liberal Protestant scholars believed that when this process of piercing through the creeds, of dismantling dogmatic accretions upon the original Jesus, was complete, they would be presented with a recognisable, reliable portrait of the real Jesus, and were confident that he could form a permanent basis for a reconstructed version of Christianity. They were fond of contrasting the religion *about* Jesus, which they viewed with suspicion, with the religion *of* Jesus, which was the true basis and origin of Christianity.'[8]

This quest for the Jesus of history has today largely been abandoned as a failure. This is partly because of the attitude of mind which underlay the quest, and partly because of the nature of the Gospel records. The older Liberal theologians began with an *a priori* rejection of everything miraculous; so they believed they could reconstruct a historical Jesus by

---

[5] *Ibid.*, p. 137.        [6] *Ibid.*, p. 127.

[7] *Cf.* C. F. D. Moule, *The Phenomenon of the New Testament*, pp. 44ff.

[8] Anthony Hanson (Editor), *Vindications: Essays on the Historical Basis of Christianity* (SCM Press, 1966), p. 29.

discarding all the supernatural elements in the Gospels. But this attempt was doomed to failure, for they found that the miracles were so intertwined with the teaching, and the supernatural with the natural, that they could not discard the one and retain the other. [9]

The Gospels on their part, moreover, were never intended to provide the material for a biography of Jesus. They are not meant to give a 'Life of Jesus' as such, or to provide the data for a complete and detached historical documentation. They are basically a proclamation of good news: good news about one whom the writers had come to believe in as God's final self-revelation to man. They cannot – and do not – claim to be dispassionate historical records written in a spirit of purely objective enquiry.

More recently, therefore, the tendency has been to put the emphasis almost exclusively on the Lord of faith rather than the Jesus of history. Rudolf Bultmann, for example, has maintained that the historical enquirer can be sure of little more about the latter than that 'a man called Jesus of Nazareth really lived; and that the Church, which lives by faith in the exalted Christ, needs to know no more than this basic fact, that Jesus was a person belonging to history and hence more than a mere symbol or mythical figure.' For true faith, as Otto Betz continues, 'will not rest on scientifically established, universally acceptable facts. It clings to the Word of God, which is outside human control. It is this Word alone, pro-claimed by the New Testament Church, which leads us to the crucified and risen Lord. The statement that Jesus of Nazareth is the Christ, the Saviour of mankind, cannot be demonstrated as a general and inevitable truth. It only becomes true in the venture of faith, the venture of a free, personal decision.'[1]

But on that basis we should be faced with only two alter-natives. We should either have to choose the existentialist road, preach the 'Christ event', and challenge our fellow-men to make an act of faith in Christ virtually regardless of any historical foundation; or we should have to accept the church's interpretation of Jesus as authoritative, and leave it at that. But the church has never had the right to demand an unquestioning acceptance of all its assertions about Christ. 'On the contrary,' as R. P. C. Hanson says, 'the Church from the earliest period has produced historical evidence to support its claim without ever maintaining that historical evidence alone was enough. . . . We must therefore conclude *neither* that Christian belief is totally emancipated from a consideration of historical evidence, *nor* that the truth of Christianity rests, or can be made to rest, on historical evidence alone. In other words, the term "the Christ of the *kerygma*"[2] is a meaningless statement, void of content, if we refuse to regard any historical evidence about Christ as relevant to it; and at the same time any historical evidence about Christ which we may collect, even the fullest and most circumstantial and best established, can go no further than producing some of the materials for Christian belief, but cannot itself afford the sole basis for this belief.'[3]

The fact is that both those who followed the quest for the Jesus of history as distinct from the Christ of the apostolic proclamation and those who concentrate today almost exclusively on the Lord of faith are postulating far too wide and unbridgeable a gulf between the two. The more extreme exponents of what is known as Form Criticism go so far as to maintain that the material in the Gospels has been so moulded and adapted by the primitive church that no purely historical figure can be identified; but some of the disciples of Bultmann have themselves recognized that they are in danger, at this point, of 'losing themselves in a world of myth and make-believe'. Gunther Bornkamm, for instance, says that we must look for the history in the *kerygma* and that we should not be resigned or sceptical about the historical Jesus. It is in this context that Dr John Macquarrie writes: 'My own view is that the Christian theologian needs to assert a minimal core of factual history if the *kerygma* is to present us with a way of life that is realistic and not culled from a dream world. This minimal core is not a short list of essential incidents or sayings, but simply the assertion that at the source of the Christian religion there was an actual historical instance of the pattern of life proclaimed in the *kerygma*.'[4]

---

[2] *I.e.* the 'proclamation' of the apostolic church.        [3] *Vindications*, p. 67.
[4] 'History and the Life of Faith', *The Listener*, 12 April 1962.

This, as it seems to me, is quite inadequate. But it at least recognizes the inescapable fact that the *kerygma* must have been based on a real, historical person, who had actually – and *very* recently – lived a life of the unique quality to which the *kerygma* called men. It is significant that W. Pannenberg, with his very radical approach to the Gospels, unhesitatingly asserts that 'recent study of Jesus has shown, with general agreement, that ... the claim of Jesus himself, which is implicitly contained not only in his message but in his whole work, precedes the faith of the disciples'.[5] This is not the place to embark on a consideration of the date at which each of the Gospels was written, or the manner of their composition, were this within my competence; but I am convinced that we must reject the view that they were not intended to stand up to historical investigation. They were, no doubt, written as testimonies of faith rather than cold history. But each of them portrays Jesus as a real, historical person, as no-one who reads them objectively can doubt. In their present form they were almost certainly compiled at a later date than several of the Epistles, although a comparatively formalized oral tradition and various written sources probably go back to the very beginning. But the attempt to date the Gospels as they now exist a century or more after the events they record has definitely failed, crushed under a weight of contrary evidence. The Evangelists, as Otto Betz observes, stand in a double relationship to Christ – both horizontal and vertical: 'On the one hand through the current of tradition, which carried the words and acts of the earthly Jesus to them; on the other through faith in the heavenly Christ, present in the preached word, in the Holy Spirit and in the sacraments. The modern distinction between Jesus as a historical figure and Christ as a historical force did not exist for them.'[6]

Now the attitude of the apostolic church and the content of the apostolic confession can be readily ascertained from documents of indisputable authority. I have already referred to the fact that no competent scholar today questions the Pauline authorship of 1 Corinthians or that it was written between AD 52 and 57. But the apostle tells us in 15:3, first,

[5] *Jesus – God and Man* (SCM Press, 1968), p. 54.
[6] *What do we know about Jesus?*, pp. 7, 11.

that he had already given his readers an account by word of
mouth of what he was now committing to paper (and that
would take us back to AD 50 or 51), and then that he had
himself received it as a tradition from those who were apostles
before him. This would certainly take us back to AD 35 or
soon after, when he paid the visit to Jerusalem about which
he tells us in Galatians 1; and it is significant that he records
in this chapter a private appearance of the risen Christ to
both Peter and James, the only two apostles whom he met
on that occasion. It is probable, however, that he in fact
received the substance of this tradition from Ananias and the
Christians at Damascus immediately after his own conversion.[7]
In any case, he tells us explicitly in 15:11 that this was no
private proclamation of his own but the common tradition,
and the very heart of the proclamation, of the apostolic
church; and this chapter seems to prove that it was firmly
established within a decade – at the very most – after the
crucifixion.[8]

The substance of this tradition is the terse statement, the
very structure and wording of which suggests a credal formula, that 'Christ died for our sins in accordance with the
scriptures, that he was buried, that he was raised on the third
day in accordance with the scriptures'.[9] But it is significant
that this is immediately supported by the unequivocal assertion
that the risen Christ was not only seen by Peter, James and the
other apostles, but, on one occasion, by more than five
hundred Christians at once, the majority of whom were still
alive when this letter was written. So this is a piece of historical
evidence of outstanding importance. We know who wrote it,
approximately when he wrote it, and the way in which he
exposed himself to contradiction and criticism if what he
wrote was not in accordance with the testimony of the many
eyewitnesses who were still alive.

It is also significant that in this same Epistle we have a
verse which echoes the teaching of the prologue to John's
Gospel. In the context of a discussion about food offered to

---

[7] Cf. A. M. Hunter, *Paul and his Predecessors* (SCM Press, 1961), pp. 15–18.
[8] W. Pannenberg argues that the credal formula quoted here 'must have
reached back to the first five years after Jesus' death' (*Jesus – God and Man*,
p. 90).                                    [9] 1 Cor. 15:3, 4.

idols the apostle states that 'for us there is one God, the Father, from whom are all things and for whom we exist, and one Lord, Jesus Christ, through whom are all things and through whom we exist'.[1] This is virtually indistinguishable from John's affirmation that 'In the beginning was the Word, and the Word was with God, and the Word was God. He was in the beginning with God; all things were made through him, and without him was not anything made that was made'[2] – except that here Paul makes no distinction whatever between the pre-incarnate Word and the incarnate Christ. And in the Epistle to the Romans – again accepted by all scholars as indisputably Pauline – the apostle summarizes the gospel he had been commissioned to preach by stating that the Jesus of history, 'a descendant of David by human genealogy',[3] had been declared to be the Son of God 'by a mighty act in that he rose from the dead'.[4] This is the very sum and substance of the apostolic *kerygma* as this is summarized in the speeches attributed to Peter and Paul in the Acts of the Apostles.

Even if we confine ourselves to those Epistles which are indubitably Pauline, there are many passing references to the facts recorded in the Gospels. It is clear that to Paul Jesus was a real man, 'born of woman, born under the law'[5] and, as we have seen, of Davidic stock.[6] His 'meekness and gentleness'[7] were matters of common knowledge, yet he was 'betrayed'[8] and crucified by the rulers of this world,[9] the Jews themselves being basically responsible.[1] The Last Supper is recounted at some length.[2] There are also echoes of the teaching of Jesus – *e.g.* in the apostle's emphasis on love as fulfilling the law,[3] and on paying tribute to those to whom it is due.[4] In regard to marriage, moreover, the apostle carefully distinguishes between the commandment of the Lord and his own judgment.[5] It has been justly remarked that 'The

[1] 1 Cor. 8:6.   [2] Jn. 1:1-3.
[3] Rom. 1:3, J. B. Phillips' translation.
[4] Rom. 1:4, NEB.   [5] Gal. 4:4.   [6] Rom. 1:3.
[7] 2 Cor. 10:1.   [8] 1 Cor. 11:23.   [9] 1 Cor. 2:8.
[1] 1 Thes. 2:15.   [2] 1 Cor. 11:23-26.
[3] Rom. 13:10; Gal. 5:14.
[4] Rom. 13:7; Mk. 12:7; for these references *cf.* R. Dunkerley, *Beyond the Gospels*, pp. 17ff.   [5] 1 Cor. 7:10-12, 25.

charge of Paul being "the great innovator" (or the great corrupter) of the Gospel must be dropped for good and all. Original Paul was, but the thing about which he wrote with such individual and creative power was not his own discovery or invention. It was the common tradition of the Christian faith which he took over from those who were "in Christ" before him. Is not this a conclusion of quite capital importance?'[6]

The Petrine authorship of 1 Peter has been much debated, the chief argument to the contrary being the quality of the Greek. But it would seem very possible that it was in fact Silvanus (probably to be identified with the Silas of Acts 15 and 16, and a New Testament 'prophet' in his own right) who actually wrote it down; and there are excellent grounds for believing that the apostle Peter was its real author.[7] The letter certainly includes a number of natural, unselfconscious touches which seem to indicate the testimony of an eyewitness and would be particularly appropriate to Peter. It refers to the sinlessness of Christ,[8] his role as Shepherd of his people,[9] his patience and forbearance at his trial,[1] his sufferings,[2] his atoning death[3] and his promised glory.[4] It is also significant that the meaning of the crucifixion is explained by reference to precisely the same chapter in the Old Testament as that to which Luke tells us that Jesus himself referred on the way to the garden of Gethsemane.[5] And the author of 1 John bases his whole message on 'that . . . which we have heard, which we have seen with our eyes, which we have looked upon and touched with our hands' (changing abruptly, in these two phrases, to the aorist of an historical event) – for the Word of life, he says, was actually 'made manifest, and we saw it, and testify to it'.[6]

So much for the Epistles. But this lightning survey not only serves to substantiate the summary of the teaching of the primitive church with which our consideration of the testimony of the New Testament began, but also to show that this

[6] A. M. Hunter, *Paul and his Predecessors*, p. 150.
[7] E. G. Selwyn, *The First Epistle of St Peter* (Macmillan, 1946), pp. 7–17.
[8] 1 Pet. 2:22.                    [9] 2:35; 5:4.
[1] 2:23.          [2] 1:11.          [3] 2:24.          [4] 1:11.
[5] 2:24, 25; *cf*. Lk. 22:37.          [6] 1 Jn. 1:1, 2.

teaching included much of the material recorded in the Gospels. Surely, then, we have a right to ask, with Professor Moule, whether these apostolic confessions were justified, whether they were based on any adequate foundation, and what can be reconstructed by deductions from them. And he tells us that the answers to these questions seem, in certain quarters, to be beginning to be, 'Yes, the apostolic confessions are justified, because the figure which emerges from the most radically critical attempt at reconstruction is the figure of one whose teaching and message were of the very same quality as attaches to the figure of the apostolic proclamation. The Jesus retrieved by the most careful criticism (and it is, I think, perverse to assert that such critical reconstruction can accomplish nothing) is no longer the rationally acceptable moralist of Liberal Protestants, but a "catalyst" – a person whose very presence precipitates a crisis of faith and forces "existential" decision. . . . Thus, qualify the statement as one may (and, indeed, must), it is true that some not inconsiderable groups of scholars are daring once more, in a sense, to look back to the Jesus of history; but now they are finding, not the Liberal Protestant figure but a figure as challenging, as supernatural, as divine as is on the hither side in the apostolic Gospel.'[7]

D. E. Nineham, too, whose attachment to Form Criticism is well known, summarizes the position, as he sees it, when he says: 'As we have seen, it is possible to some extent to reconstruct the units of tradition on which the gospels are based. When we do reconstruct them, not only do we find that the units on which St Mark is based presuppose *broadly* the same Christ as the finished Gospel, but we find that other units, preserved independently in other places and used by the other evangelists, also preserve a fundamentally similar figure. Our basic picture of Christ is thus carried back to a point only a quarter of a century or so after his death; and when we bear in mind the wonderfully retentive memory of the Oriental, who, being unable to read and write, had perforce to cultivate accuracy of memory, it will not seem surprising that we can often be virtually sure that what the tradition is offering us

---

[7] *The Phenomenon of the New Testament*, pp. 46f.

are the authentic deeds, and especially the authentic words, of the historic Jesus.'[8]

Nor is this any mere generalization. On the contrary, A. M. Ramsey, Betz, Moule and other scholars refer to point after point in the Gospel records which stand up, in their view, to the most radical criticism. Betz, for example, mentions *inter alia* the parables, the proclamation of the kingdom, the teaching about the sabbath, the disputes with the Pharisees and Sadducees, the miracles and the Messianic consciousness and confession of the Jesus of the synoptic Gospels.[9] Similarly, Moule reminds us that 'what the apostles remembered of Jesus' ministry included his own interpretation of it, however much and however often this had, at the time, been misunderstood. In a sense, the post-Easter *interpretation* was only a *rediscovery* of what had been there in the teaching of Jesus himself'[1] – and he demonstrates that Luke in his Gospel does *not* 'attribute to the participants in his story of the ministry of Jesus the same explicit estimate of Jesus as he attributes to the apostles when they are speaking of the risen Jesus' in the Acts. On the contrary, he 'represents the contemporaries of Jesus in his earthly life as speaking of him with reserve. They do not use the great Christological titles of the post-resurrection preaching. Yet, equally, Luke leaves not a shadow of doubt that the one to whom the exalted titles of the Church's proclamation are applied is the same man, Jesus of Nazareth, about whom he tells us in his Gospel.'[2]

He also mentions a number of features in the tradition which survived, and were faithfully recorded, in spite of a tendency in its transmitters which would militate against them or the fact that the evangelists themselves do not seem to have grasped their significance. Examples of such features can be found in Jesus' attitude to, and relations with, women;[3] his mission to Israel; the retention of the Semitic 'Amen' to introduce some of his statements, in a way without parallel

[8] D. E. Nineham, *Commentary on St Mark* (Penguin Books, 1963), quoted in A. M. Ramsey, *God, Christ and the World* (SCM Press, 1969), pp. 74f.

[9] *What do we know about Jesus?*, pp. 48ff. (and p. 34), p. 32, pp. 78ff., pp. 58ff. and pp. 83ff. respectively.

[1] *The Phenomenon of the New Testament*, p. 46 (citing, in part, O. Cullmann).

[2] *Ibid.*, pp. 57f.

[3] See further under chapter 2 on this point.

in rabbinic usage, because (as Käsemann puts it) 'in his person and words the Kingdom of God manifested its presence and authority'; his identification of John the Baptist with Elijah; and his association of baptism with teaching about death and resurrection.[4] All this, he says, gives the lie, on the one hand, 'to the notion that the Church's estimate of Jesus is something which Christians unconsciously adopted in the course of time, and then simply assumed as having obtained from the beginning'. Similarly, those aspects of Jesus' attitude and ministry which have survived in the traditions, despite the fact that the early Christians do not seem to have paid any particular attention to them or to have recognized their Christological significance, 'bear witness in a subtle and paradoxical way to the identity of the Jesus of the ministry with the Lord who was worshipped, and to the tenacity and continuity of the traditions about him.'[5]

The conclusion that the primitive church did not exercise anything approaching the creative influence over the material we find in the Gospels as is postulated by the more extreme Form Critics is reinforced by the sharp divisions between them on point after point in their attempted reconstructions. Their methods strike the lawyer as basically more subjective than objective, for every scholar seems to make a different selection of so-called facts, and then dub the rest fancy. 'The inevitable result', as R. P. C. Hanson says, 'is that all the facts might as well be fancy because, while it is agreed that *some* of them are almost certainly facts, nobody can produce any satisfactory reason why his selection should be regarded as facts and not fancy, rather than that one, or that one, or that one. It is not merely that every critic plays the game differently from the others, but that every critic makes his own rules.'[6]

It is interesting in this context to see how a classical scholar such as A. N. Sherwin-White regards the scepticism of many New Testament critics, and how strange he finds their attitude when compared with that of those scholars who examine the history of a variety of classical figures whose acts and words are considerably less well-documented. And his own examina-

---

[4] *The Phenomenon of the New Testament*, pp. 63–73.
[5] *Ibid.*, pp. 75ff.　　　　　　　[6] *Vindications*, p. 30.

B

tion of the New Testament material in the light of Roman law and customs is, I think, of considerable significance.[7]

For myself, then, I stand unhesitatingly with Professor Moule when he says that 'the alternatives are not either mere history coupled with a rationalistic estimate of Jesus as a very good man (an estimate such as could be made by an atheist), or commitment to a preached but unauthenticated Lord. . . . The creed is not a series of assertions made in a vacuum, but a summary of value-judgements reached on the basis of eye-witness testimony to an event.'[8] Put somewhat differently, we must agree with Otto Betz that to accept Jesus' Messianic claim – with all that this involves – is an act of faith. 'But it is not conjured up out of nothing; it is based on history. It is the "yes" of faith to the claim of a historical personage. Apart from such an assent there is only the decisive "no" which is a denial of Jesus' messianic claim. It is the "no" of Caiaphas and the Jews in Jerusalem. There is no third possibility. For whoever sees in Jesus the wandering rabbi, the proclaimer of the end of the world or the witness of faith, falls short of his own claim and the testimony of his disciples.'[9]

But not only do the Gospels bear their testimony to the unique figure which dominates their pages – which will, in large part, be the subject of the next chapter – but the unique figure himself may be said to authenticate the Gospels. It was John Stuart Mill who said: 'It is of no use to say that Christ, as exhibited in the Gospels, is not historical, and that we know not how much of what is admirable has been super-added by the tradition of his followers. Who among his disciples or among their proselytes was capable of inventing the sayings of Jesus or of imagining the life and character revealed in the Gospels? Certainly not the fishermen of Galilee; as certainly not St Paul, whose character and idiosyncrasies were of a totally different sort; still less the early Christian writers, in whom nothing is more evident than that the good which was in them was all derived, as they always professed that it was derived, from the higher source.'[1]

[7] A. N. Sherwin-White, *Roman Society and Roman Law in the New Testament* (Oxford University Press, 1963).
[8] Moule, *op. cit.*, p. 79.          [9] *What do we know about Jesus?*, p. 114.
[1] John Stuart Mill, *Three Essays on Religion* (London, 1874), pp. 253f.

Nor is this argument weakened by the fact that the writers
the Gospels relied, to a considerable extent, on oral tradi-
on and written records (including, of course, the inter-
ependence, in part, of the Synoptic Gospels). The more
emplex the origin of the Gospels and the more numerous
te strata of their sources, the greater the problem of the
ortrait they paint.[2] As Rousseau justly remarked: 'It is more
conceivable that several men should have united to forge
te Gospel than that a single person should have furnished
te subject of it. The Gospel has marks of truth so great, so
riking, so perfectly inimitable, that the inventor of it would
e more astonishing than the hero.'[3]

The force of this argument is immensely increased when we
ompare the four canonical Gospels – all of which were
most certainly composed, in their present form, between
o 65 and the end of the first century – with the apocryphal
ospels of a century later. 'All who read them with any
tention', says B. Harris Cowper in the preface to his Trans-
tion, 'will see that they are fictions, and not histories, not
aditions even, so much as legends'; and he adds: 'Before I
ndertook this work I never realised so completely as I do
ow the impassable character of the gulf which separates the
enuine Gospels from these.'[4]

It is interesting to compare this statement with the testi-
ony of two men who have recently translated the canonical
ospels into colloquial English. 'I have read, in Greek and
atin, scores of myths,' writes J. B. Phillips, 'but I did not find
e slightest flavour of myth here. . . . One sensed again and
rain that understatement which we have been taught to
ink is more "British" than Oriental.' And Phillips recounts
at Dr E. V. Rieu, a leading classical scholar who undertook
e task of translating the Gospels because he had an intense
esire to satisfy himself about their authenticity, testified that
e found the whole material extraordinarily alive. 'It changed

f. W. H. Griffith Thomas, *Christianity is Christ* (Church Book Room Press,
46 edition), p. 71.

ee W. Robertson Nicoll, *The Church's One Foundation* (Hodder and
ughton, 1901), p. 41.

. Harris Cowper, Preface to *The Apocryphal Gospels and other Documents
ating to the History of Christ* (Williams and Norgate, 1867).

me', he said. 'My work changed me. And I came to th
conclusion that these words bear the seal of the Son of Ma·
and God.'[5]

In the following chapters I shall base my conclusions abou
the person of Christ, the meaning of his death and the his
toricity of his resurrection on the New Testament as a whole
without more than a few passing references to whether th
relevant evidence is derived from the Synoptic Gospels, th
Fourth Gospel, those Epistles which are indubitably Pauline
or elsewhere. Professor Moule has argued persuasivel
'that all four Gospels alike are to be interpreted as more tha
anything else evangelistic and apologetic in purpose; and tha
the Synoptic Gospels represent primarily the recognitio
that a vital element in evangelism is the plain story of wha
happened in the ministry of Jesus.'[6] The Fourth Gospel clearl
includes a much more extensive interpretative element; bu
recent studies have shown how primitive and Palestinian
its background, and who are we to interpret the life an
teachings of Jesus compared with the 'beloved disciple', t
whom the record (even if not the Gospel in its final form) i
my belief assuredly goes back?[7] As for the apostolic testimon·
we have discussed the authority and exceedingly early da·
of some of the Epistles, and the remaining books of the Ne
Testament do not differ from these at all significantly in the
teaching. It is a strangely perverse attitude, as Profess·
Moule has remarked, 'which, while quite unwarrantabl
hospitable to the latest irresponsible speculation by journalist
charlatans, insists on treating such serious documents a
those which comprise the New Testament as though they ha
long ago been discredited.'[8]

But there is another vital factor in all this – the claim of th
Bible to divine inspiration. We shall see in the next chapter tha
there can be no doubt – unless we are to make complete no·
sense of the Gospels – that Christ himself paid repeate
testimony to the divine authority of the Old Testame·

[5] J. B. Phillips, *Ring of Truth* (Hodder and Stoughton, 1967), pp. 57f.;
E. M. Blaiklock, *Layman's Answer*, p. 44.
[6] *The Phenomenon of the New Testament*, p. 113.
[7] *Cf.* William Temple, *Readings in St. John's Gospel* (Macmillan, 1949), p
x and xvi.    [8] *The Phenomenon of the New Testament*, p. 2.

It is noteworthy in this context what an impact Christ has made on a wide variety of men and women all down the ages. Even agnostics have not infrequently paid their tribute. 'Rest now in thy glory, noble founder,' wrote Renan. 'Thy work is completed, thy divinity is established. . . . Between thee and God men will no longer distinguish. Complete vanquisher of death, take possession of thy kingdom.'[1] 'Can the Person whose history the Gospels relate be himself a man?' asked Rousseau. '. . . What sublimity in his maxims! What profound wisdom in his discourses! What presence of mind, what ingenuity of justice in his replies! Yes, if the life and death of Socrates are those of a philosopher, the life and death of Jesus Christ are those of a God.'[2]

Similar tributes have been paid by many others who may or may not have professed any personal allegiance to him. Speaking of Alexander, Caesar, Charlemagne and himself, Napoleon wrote: 'I think I understand something of human nature; and I tell you, all these were men, and I am a man: none else is like Him; Jesus Christ was more than a man.'[3] And it is in a similar vein that Raymond Fletcher, an agnostic Member of Parliament and himself an author, wrote in *The Guardian*[4] that Christians do not 'need miracles to sustain their beliefs. Christ himself was the miracle'.

But it is in the teaching of the apostolic church, rather than the tributes paid by later generations, that we must find our starting-point in our present study. As we noted in the previous chapter, there can be no doubt whatever that, from an exceedingly early date, the apostles and their immediate entourage proclaimed him not merely as the Jewish Messiah but as the pre-existent Word or Son of God, the very agent of creation, eternally one with the Father, who 'came down' from heaven and was 'made man'. So perfectly did he reveal God that he could be described as the 'image' of the invisible God, in whom alone the Godhead could be seen by mortal eyes.[5] Nor did he stop at becoming man; he identified himself

[1] *La Vie de Jésus*, quoted by E. M. Blaiklock, *Layman's Answer*, pp. 30ff.
[2] Quoted by Frank Ballard, *The Miracles of Unbelief* (T. and T. Clark, 1913), p. 251.
[3] Quoted by H. P. Liddon, *The Divinity of our Lord* (Rivington, 1889), p. 150.
[4] 23 December 1968.          [5] *Cf.* Col. 1:15; Heb. 1:3.

with men and women in their sin and spiritual bankruptcy
so completely that on the cross he was even 'made sin' to
redeem us and reconcile us to God.[6] He died in apparent
weakness, but God vindicated him and raised him from the
dead; and he now sits on the throne of the universe, awaiting
the day when he will again appear to human eyes – not in
weakness but in power, not to suffer but to reign, not as
redeemer but as judge of men.

It is our task in this present chapter to submit this belief of
the primitive church to such examination as we can. How far
does it really accord with the picture which emerges from a
study of the Gospels? Is this picture itself demonstrably
false or inconsistent, or does it stand up to criticism? Does it
derive any support from the Old Testament, or from a
fuller consideration of the way in which the apostolic church
interpreted and understood it? And what, if this picture is to
be accepted, are its necessary implications?

But before we turn to these questions a few remarks must be
made by way of clearing the ground. When the primitive
church spoke of Christ as coming down from heaven at the
incarnation, and of ascending again after the resurrection,
was it guilty of an almost infantile naïvety? Was it obsessed
with the concept of a flat earth and a God who was somehow
poised above it? If so, does not the whole idea become
meaningless now that we know that the earth is round, and
that what is 'up' in Europe is 'down' in Australia? Would it
be better to discard any idea of 'up there' and substitute some
such phrase as 'out there'? But even this would seem to point
in some definite direction and indicate some geographical
locality, wherever it might be. Is it not time, therefore, for us
not only to abandon such picture language, but also the
theological concepts which lie behind them?

I must confess that it seems to me that those who object
to this language are themselves somewhat naïve. I doubt if
there are many literate adults today who do not realize that
what is 'up' in one hemisphere is necessarily 'down' in the
other, whatever language they may use; nor do I believe that
most people think of 'heaven' as situated in some particular
direction. To teach the young to sing about the 'Friend for

[6] 2 Cor. 5:21.

little children, above the bright blue sky' may be open to objection, but what we really mean when we talk of God being 'up there' or 'out there' is that God is transcendent as well as immanent. When we say that Christ 'came down'[7] from heaven at the incarnation we mean that he came from the transcendent world into the world of men which he had created; and when we say that he ascended up into heaven we mean that he went back to the Godhead. To the eyes of the disciples the Lord who ascended necessarily went 'up'. To ask if heaven is a place, moreover, is to beg the question, for it necessarily depends on the content given to the word 'place'. The fact is that we are dealing, in all these matters, with concepts beyond human speech or analysis, and that all we can hope to do is to use metaphors and picture language. But to say this is not to imply that such language is meaningless, or even naïve. The metaphors of one age may not altogether suit the idiom, or the knowledge, of another; but they still describe the same realities, even if the terminology must sometimes be changed.

But the emphasis placed by the Creeds on the fact that Christ came to this world of men from outside humanity, and that he returned after the resurrection to the transcendent world, does not mean that the incarnation was a mere 'theophany', or that Christ simply assumed a human body for the duration of his earthly life. The Christian doctrine of the incarnation is that Christ became man in a much deeper sense than this, and that he is truly man as well as truly God. We shall be concerned with the evidence for, and with some of the implications of, this doctrine later in this chapter. For the present it must suffice to say that to deny his true humanity is as much a heresy as to deny his deity, for it is heresy to emphasize one aspect of the truth in such a way as to distort the unity and balance of the whole.

When we turn to the Gospels there can be no doubt whatever about the true humanity of the central figure. He was born as a helpless baby; he grew 'in wisdom and stature'; and he experienced hunger, thirst, weariness, pain and death. He could be both angry and deeply grieved; he could be moved with compassion; he asked questions because he

[7] *Cf.* Jn. 6:33, 38.

wanted to know the answers, and, on one occasion, frankly
admitted that there were limits to his knowledge; and he could
feel a natural affinity with particular individuals. It is true
that we never read of him as laughing, and that the picture
we get is of one so deeply conscious of the sins and sorrows of
humanity, and so absorbed in doing his Father's will, that he
had little time for the lighter side of life. Yet he loved children;
he was the 'friend of publicans and sinners'; he prayed that his
disciples might share the joy he knew; and it seems inescapable
to me that some of the statements he is recorded as having
made must have been accompanied by a smile and a flash
of humour. And while the title by which he most frequently,
as it seems, referred to himself – Son of man – may have had a
Messianic content, I feel sure he intended it also to emphasize
his identification with those whose nature he shared.

Yet the Gospels equally obviously depict him as unique.
This is shown in his teaching, his miracles, his sinlessness, his
claims and his resurrection. The last of these will be the
subject of the fourth chapter; but we must consider the other
four in turn. He was unique, first, in his teaching – if we take
it in its width, its scope and its confident certainty. What seems
to have most impressed his immediate hearers was, indeed, the
authority with which he, unlearned as he was in the technical
learning of the schools, spoke about God and man, heaven and
earth – and this 'extraordinary sense of personal authority'[8]
has been singled out by several modern critics as one of the
most remarkable and unmistakably historical features in the
Gospels. But today the ordinary reader is, perhaps, even more
impressed that not one of the sayings attributed to him has
become outdated by the passage of the years, has been proved
false, or has lost its point or pungency when transported into
entirely different environments. He was, moreover, remarkably outspoken: he could refer to Herod the tetrarch as 'that
fox', and his compassion for the weak and erring went hand in
hand with the most scathing denunciations of religious hypo-
crites. To think of him only as 'gentle Jesus, meek and mild'
is a caricature.

The parables in which he couched so much of his teaching

[8] *Cf.* C. F. D. Moule, *The Phenomenon of the New Testament*, pp. 67f., citing E.
Käsemann, C. E. Ladd and H. Schlier.

are outstanding for their originality as well as their spiritual insight. It may be true that there is little in his moral teaching which is wholly original; for if the truth had been said before he could only repeat it, giving it his own distinctive emphasis and application. But he was radical in his approach to the oral law or 'tradition of the elders', with his unfailing emphasis on a purity which was inward and moral rather than outward and ceremonial, and his condemnation of the sins of thought and desire as well as those of word and act. Yet the astounding element in his teaching was that he was himself the very centre of his message. Others have called men to follow them through sweat, toil and blood; and other religious teachers have pointed men away from themselves to God. But he could say that 'he who loves father or mother more than me is not worthy of me'[9] and that 'he who loses his life for my sake will find it';[1] he could say, 'Come to me, all who labour and are heavy laden. . . . Take my yoke upon you, and learn from me; for I am gentle and lowly in heart.'[2] 'Gentle and lowly?' one might ask; it scarcely seems so. If that is humility, then what is pride? Yet it is plain from the New Testament that this was indeed the impression that he made on his disciples, for the apostle Paul wrote of the 'meekness and gentleness of Christ',[3] in spite of the fact that he taught in the most forthright terms that men's eternal destiny depended on their relationship to him.

We must also consider the miracles which he is said to have performed. It is right, I think, to approach anything outside the uniformity of the ordinary course of nature, as we know it, with a basic scepticism. But Dr Orr has pertinently remarked that 'The question is not, Do natural causes operate uniformly? but, Are natural causes the only causes that exist or operate? For miracle, as has frequently been pointed out, is precisely the assertion of the interposition of a *new* cause; one, besides, which the theist must admit to be a *vera causa*.'[4] The question that arises from the Gospel records, therefore, is not 'Could these miracles have been performed?' but, 'Is there sufficient evidence that they were in fact performed?' A general answer to this question is that any attempt to re-write the Gospels

[9] Mt. 10:37.　　[1] Mt. 10:39.　　[2] Mt. 11:28.　　[3] 2 Cor. 10:1.
[4] *The Resurrection of Jesus* (Hodder and Stoughton, 1908), p. 51.

without the miraculous element would be doomed to failure. The more one studies the Gospels the more apparent it becomes that the 'indissoluble connexion between the works and the words of Jesus, between these and his character and consciousness must receive due regard. The narratives of miracles are woven into the very texture of the evangelical record. How many of the sayings of Jesus are closely linked with works of healing? How many of the most beautiful and attractive traits in the portrait of Jesus are drawn from his dealing with sufferers who came to him for relief?'[5] To subtract the miraculous would emasculate the whole story and make many of its incidents – and, indeed, the reaction of the Jewish people and their leaders – inexplicable and meaningless.

Now it is true that today – in contradistinction to past centuries – miracles, by themselves, are regarded as having little evidential value, for they can be explained in a variety of different ways. It is also clear from the Gospel records, I think, that Jesus consistently refused to perform any miracle to convince a sceptic or titillate the fancy of a religious dilettante. Time and again, it was his deep compassion for human sorrow and pain which prompted his works of love and mercy; but it seems that he also, on occasions, performed miracles to confirm the faith of those who already believed, but whose faith was in need of such confirmation. It has been justly remarked that 'Miracles or signs are more properly in their highest form the substance than the proofs of revelation – The best idea which we can form of a miracle is that of an event or phenomenon which is fitted to suggest to us the action of a personal spiritual power. . . . Its essence lies not so much in what it is in itself as in what it is calculated to indicate. . . . We are not then justified either by reason or by Scripture in assigning to miracles, and still less to the record of miracles, a supreme power of proof. But none the less they fulfil externally an important function in the Divine economy. They are fitted to awaken, to arouse, to arrest the faith which is latent. They bring men who already believe in God into His Presence. They place them in an attitude of reverent expectation.'[6]

[5] A. E. Garvie, *Studies in the Inner Life of Jesus* (Hodder and Stoughton, 1907), p. 51
[6] B. F. Westcott, *The Gospel of Life* (Macmillan, 1892), pp. 206, 224.

It is unlikely, then, that many people today will come to faith in Christ primarily because of the miracles recorded in the Gospels. But if they come to believe in him as the incarnate Son of God on other grounds, they will not be at all surprised to read that he opened blind eyes and deaf ears; that he made the lame walk, the bowed stand upright and the paralytic whole; and even that he raised the dead. These miracles in the sphere of physical life and health were but signs of his spiritual power – as was also his authority over inanimate nature. It has been justly said that 'The miracles are harmonious with the character and consciousness of Jesus; they are not external confirmations, but internal constituents of the revelation of the Heavenly Father's love, mercy and grace, given in him, the beloved Son of God, and the compassionate Brother of men'.[7] And the unique element in his miracles is that, unlike the apostles, he did not disclaim his own part in these manifestations of divine power, nor say that he had done them only in the name and authority of another.

But his miracles pale to relative insignificance beside the perfection of his character and the fact of his resurrection. The latter will be the subject of our fourth chapter, so we shall not anticipate – except to say that, if the fact of his resurrection is admitted, little difficulty need be felt in accepting any other miracle (including the virgin birth) provided it is adequately attested. What, then, are we to make of his alleged sinlessness?

Now it is true that a number of criticisms have been levelled at two or three of the incidents recorded of him and at certain elements in his teaching – and these we shall discuss later. But it is clear that the New Testament depicts him as having lived a life which was consistent through and through. 'He committed no sin',[8] 'in him there is no sin'[9] was, it seems, the testimony of his most intimate disciples. Similarly, the Fourth Gospel tells us that he challenged even his enemies to convict or convince him of sin[1] and declared that Satan had no power over him.[2] But the testimony goes much deeper than any isolated statement, for it rests on the fact that the records give no hint whatever that he had any personal consciousness of sin. As C. E. Jefferson justly remarks: 'The

[7] A. E. Garvie, op. cit., pp. 51f.
[9] 1 Jn. 3:5.       [1] Jn. 8:46.
[8] 1 Pet. 2:22.
[2] Jn. 14:30.

best reason we have for believing in the sinlessness of Jesus is the fact that He allowed His dearest friends to think that He was. There is in all His talk no trace of regret or hint of compunction, or suggestion of sorrow for shortcoming, or slightest vestige of remorse. He taught other men to think of themselves as sinners, He asserted plainly that the human heart is evil, He told His disciples that every time they prayed they were to pray to be forgiven, but He never speaks or acts as though He Himself has the slightest consciousness of having ever done anything other than what was pleasing to God.'[3]

To appreciate the full significance of this fact we must contrast the inner consciousness of Jesus with that of those men and women whom we rightly regard as saints. The further they progress in the inner life, and the nearer they get to God, the more conscious they seem to become of wrong within. Imperfections which were once tolerable or even unnoticed become black, ugly and abhorrent in the light of a deeper apprehension of the divine holiness. Yet in him there is not only a total absence of any recorded sense of sin, but 'from time to time declarations of His own holiness and meekness. There was not a trace of that self-depreciation which in others is associated with the highest character. This is all the more remarkable if we observe the instances in the life of Jesus Christ when He expressed indignation against his enemies . . . With every other man the expression of indignation tends to a subsequent feeling of compunction, or, at any rate, to a close examination whether there may not have been some elements of personal animosity or injustice in the expression of anger. But with Jesus Christ there was nothing of the kind. Not for a single instant did the faintest shadow come between Him and His heavenly Father.'[4]

All this is largely negative – the absence of sin; and it is, of course, impossible to prove a negative. We can note the failure of his opponents to bring any moral accusation against him, even at his trial; we can weigh the testimony, both explicit and implicit, of those who knew him best; and we can

---

[3] *The Character of Jesus* (Thomas Y. Crowell, 1908), p. 225.
[4] W. H. Griffith Thomas, *Christianity is Christ*, p. 16, summarizing D. W. Forrest, *The Christ of History and Experience* (T. and T. Clark, 1901), pp. 10–25.

ponder the fact that one who has, all down the ages, made other men conscious of their sins and unworthiness, seems to have had no such consciousness himself – even of forgiven sins. But could he have been so insensitive that he sinned without knowing it? Let us briefly examine some of the accusations which have been brought against him.

The incident in which he is recorded as having healed the daughter of a Syro-Phoenician woman[5] has given rise to two accusations: first, that he was narrow and race-bound in his sympathies; secondly, that he was arrogant and insensitive in his attitude towards her and in the words he used. It is certainly true that at first he appeared to be unwilling to extend his ministry of love, mercy and teaching beyond the race in which he had been born and to which he had pri-marily been sent. No doubt there is a limited sense in which this was true; he had come with a specific ministry to which he consistently gave priority. But it is perfectly clear that his sympathies flowed much more widely than this – as can be seen in the parable of the Good Samaritan;[6] in his healing of the centurion's servant, and his commendation of the former's faith;[7] in his assertion that many would come from east and west and sit down in the kingdom of heaven, while the children of the kingdom might be cast out;[8] in his refer-ence to the 'other' sheep, not of 'this fold', whom he must also win;[9] in his commission to his disciples to take his message to 'every creature' or 'the whole creation';[1] etc. Surely we are entitled to interpret a single incident – about which we have no more than a bare summary – in the light of his consistent attitude and teaching? And much the same reasoning applies to the way in which he spoke to the woman. I have little doubt, myself, that he made the remark about the children's bread and the little dogs (a diminutive in the Greek) with a smile that dissipated any apparent superiority, and that his whole intention was to draw out her faith, which he then com-mended and rewarded. One is reminded of the incident[2] in which he forced the woman healed of an 'issue of blood' to declare herself – to her immediate embarrassment but eternal profit.

I myself find more difficulty in understanding the incident

[5] Mk. 7:25–30.    [6] Lk. 10:29–37.    [7] Mt. 8:5–10.    [8] Mt. 8:11, 12.
[9] Jn. 10:16.    [1] Mk. 16:15.    [2] Mk. 5:24–34.

48      CHRISTIANITY: THE WITNESS OF HISTORY

of the Gadarene swine[3] – chiefly because most of us, at least,
are so ignorant of the whole subject of demon possession.
Missionaries are emphatic that this phenomenon still exists
today, that it is quite distinct from – although easily confused
with – psychiatric disorder, and that it should be treated in a
radically different way. It is possible that demon possession is,
in fact, more common than we realize in our own countries,
particularly among those who have dabbled in any way in
spiritism. The mystery in this particular incident is why the
demons asked to be allowed to go into the swine and why
Jesus gave them this permission. Nor can we be sure whether
he himself knew, when he gave this permission, what the
result would be – but to this question of the extent of his
supernatural knowledge we must return later. No exaggerated
sympathy need be lavished on the pigs; for they were being
raised for slaughter, and they probably had a quick death.
It is just possible, moreover, that their owners were keeping
them for trade with Jews, to whom such meat was forbidden.
But however that may be, the incident emphasizes the incomparable value of a human soul; and the request of the
owners of the pigs that Jesus should go elsewhere reflects the
way in which we ourselves so often fail to have a true per-
spective or valid scale of values.

Another charge which has been brought against the Christ
of the Gospels is that of petulance, and even vindictiveness, in
the cleansing of the Temple and the cursing of the barren
fig-tree.[4] But little difficulty need be experienced in explaining
the first of these, at any rate. No element of personal affront
to his own dignity or interests was involved. On the contrary,
his indignation was directed against the way in which the
money-changers and their fellows were putting his 'Father's
house' to a wrong use, exploiting the poor, and indulging their
own greed. Incidentally, the record does not necessarily
suggest that the 'whip of cords' was used for any other purpose
than driving the animals out of the Temple; and it is a little
curious that this incident is sometimes quoted as a blemish
in his moral character by the very people who also complain,
in effect, that he was weak and ineffective.

The case of the barren fig-tree is rather different. Discussion

[3] Mt. 8:28–34.      [4] Jn. 2:14–16; Mk. 11:12–14, 20.

of this incident has been confused by the vexed question of whether winter figs can be found on a tree when the time for the new crop has not yet come, or whether the leaves which normally indicate the presence of fruit were themselves, in this case, premature and unnatural; but surely we are entitled to assume that anyone brought up in the country, and with the knowledge of nature which Jesus so frequently revealed, would not have been petulant – a word which in any case seems singularly out of character – had the presence of any sort of fruit been impossible. No, the incident must surely be interpreted as an enacted parable of judgment. The fig-tree, like Israel then and so many of us today, gave the appearance of fruitfulness when it was in fact barren. But God is concerned with facts, not show – and those who display a piety which is not real are always in danger of his judgment. Thus the cursing of the fig-tree, and the way in which it withered and died, vividly portray the fate which awaits religious hypocrisy. But it is surely noteworthy that the object of this one and only enacted parable of judgment was not a man, nor an animal, but a tree.

But was Jesus right to believe – as he certainly did – in a God who loved sinners but hated their sin; in a God who was 'light', in the sense of utter moral purity, as well as 'love'; in a God who was willing to go to incredible lengths to save men from misery and sin, but who was none the less the righteous judge who could not ignore evil? It is clear from the Gospels that Jesus not infrequently spoke in terms of both judgment and hell, and it is recorded in Matthew that he said he would send his angels to 'gather out of his kingdom all causes of sin and all evil-doers' and to 'throw them into the furnace of fire' where 'men will weep and gnash their teeth'[6] – and he is said to have repeated the last phrase, or something like it, on a number of occasions. But it is quite unnecessary – and in my view unjust – to conclude with Bertrand Russell that he felt 'a certain pleasure in contemplating wailing and gnashing of teeth',[7] for this would be wholly incongruous in one who had come 'to seek and to save the lost',[8] 'not to call

---

[5] 1 Jn. 1:5; 4:8.    [6] Mt. 13:41f.
[7] *Why I am not a Christian* (National Secular Society, 1967 edition), p. 9.
[8] Lk. 19:10.

the righteous, but sinners',[9] and who rejoiced so infinitely
over one lost sheep that he was able to carry safely home. No,
these and similar words were spoken, I am convinced, in sad
and solemn warning. Whether he was right to speak in that
way depends entirely, of course, on whether God is in fact a
God of judgment as well as love. And to this the whole Bible
bears consistent testimony.

Much the same considerations apply to the severity with
which he denounced the scribes and Pharisees. These denunciations were not prompted by any personal reaction to
the fact that they were so unresponsive to his teaching; they
were examples of the anger he always felt when he came
face to face with religious hypocrisy and with those who
harshly condemned in others a standard of life more excusable
than their own. It is noteworthy, moreover, that on the
occasion when the strongest expression is twice used to
describe his anger, in the incident of the raising of Lazarus,
this was caused, not by the wailing of the Jews or the conduct
of the two sisters, but by the whole phenomenon of suffering
and death.[1]

Jesus has also been accused of being ineffective,[2] in a political sense, and of having done little to right social injustices.
But it is clear from the Sermon on the Mount that he was
deeply concerned that his disciples should be both the 'salt'
and the 'light' of secular society; he endorsed the authority
of those Old Testament prophets who vehemently rebuked
social injustice; and he consistently identified himself with the
poor and weak, with social outcasts and those who were
regarded as morally disreputable. In Dietrich Bonhoeffer's
striking phrase, he was 'the man for others', who had come
not to be served but to serve, and whose basic mission was to
all who were 'lost'. It is true that he did not lead a rebellion
against Rome, seek to free slaves, or introduce a social
revolution.[3] He had come for a particular purpose, which was
far more important than any of these things – and from that

[9] Mt. 9:13.
[1] Cf. Jn. 11:33 and 38. For a fuller discussion see the next chapter (p. 75).
[2] But this was certainly not the view of the Jewish leaders, or they would
not have hounded him to the cross.
[3] But he did in fact effect almost the only revolution which can be said to
have lasted.

purpose nothing could or did deflect him. He was primarily concerned to change men as men rather than the political régime under which they lived; to transform their attitude rather than their circumstances; to treat the sickness of their hearts rather than the problems of their environment. But he laid down in a single pregnant sentence man's duty both to God and to the State when he said: 'Render to Caesar the things that are Caesar's, and to God the things that are God's'; and it is certainly not his fault that the Christian church has been so slow, down the centuries, in applying to one after another of the world's social evils the principle he emphasized so strongly, that we must love our neighbours as ourselves.

One of the most remarkable things about him was the perfect balance of character he displayed. It is a truism that a man's strong points nearly always carry with them corresponding weaknesses. He may be an extrovert or an introvert; he may be sanguine or melancholic, choleric or phlegmatic; or he may in some degree combine two or three of these temperaments. But he never succeeds in achieving a perfect balance – a sympathy which is never weak, a strength which is never insensitive, a benevolence which is never indulgent, or a drive which is never ruthless. Jesus, alone, seems to have achieved this balance; and in him every temperament finds both its ideal and its correction. He was a man, not a woman, yet women as much as men find their perfect example in him. He was a Jew, not a European, African or Indian; yet men and women of every race find in him all they would most wish to be.

One of those features which Professor Moule considers to carry the hall-mark of authenticity in the Gospels is Jesus' attitude to women and his relations with them. 'It is difficult enough for anyone, even a consummate master of imaginative writing,' he remarks, 'to create a picture of a deeply pure, good person moving about in an impure environment, without making him a prig or a prude or a sort of "plaster saint". How comes it that, through all the Gospel traditions without exception, there comes a remarkably firmly-drawn portrait of an attractive young man moving freely about among women of all sorts, including the decidedly disreputable, without a trace of sentimentality, unnaturalness, or prudery, and yet, at every point, maintaining a simple integrity of character? Is this because the environments in which the traditions were preserved and through which they were transmitted were peculiarly favourable to such a portrait? On the contrary, it seems that they were rather hostile to it.'[4]

Again, we must consider the claims he made for himself. There is the famous passage in Matthew and Luke in which he declares that 'everything has been put in my hands by my Father, and nobody knows the Son except the Father. Nor does anyone know the Father except the Son – and the man to whom the Son chooses to reveal him.' In Matthew this is immediately followed by the invitation to which passing reference has already been made: 'Come to me, all of you who are weary and overburdened, and I will give you rest! Put on my yoke and learn from me. For I am gentle and humble in heart and you will find rest for your souls. For my yoke is easy and my burden is light.'[5] These passages are almost indistinguishable from the radical statements in the Fourth Gospel which fall under such suspicion in some quarters. 'But the cumulative weight of these hints from many different levels of antiquity in the tradition', as Professor Moule puts it, 'is, I think, impressive. It looks as though here was one who perhaps seldom expressly *claimed* a title for himself except that of the suffering and eclipsed martyr Son of Man; but who *behaved* with the mastery appropriate to one who was heir to the whole Kingdom, and who occasionally lifted the veil of his self-consciousness to reveal just this at the heart of his vocation.'[6]

'I am the light of the world,' he is recorded as saying on one occasion; 'he who follows me will not walk in darkness, but will have the light of life.'[7] 'I am the bread of life,' he said at another time; 'he who comes to me shall not hunger, and he who believes in me shall never thirst.'[8] These were staggering statements. It was not that he professed to be able to shed a little illumination on the dark path of life or somewhat to dissipate the frustrations of human experience, but that he

[4] *The Phenomenon of the New Testament*, pp. 63ff.
[5] Mt. 11:27–30, J. B. Phillips' translation; *cf*. Lk. 10:22.
[6] Moule, *op. cit*, p. 53.          [7] Jn. 8:12.          [8] Jn. 6:35

asserted that he was himself both light and satisfaction and that those who really came to know him would share this light and experience this inward contentment. These sayings come from the Fourth Gospel, as does his claim to have antedated Abraham, the great founder of the Jewish race.[9] But it is in the Synoptic tradition that he is recorded as having claimed to be 'lord even of the sabbath',[1] and we know what the sabbath day meant to the Jews; that he had come 'to seek and to save the lost'[2] and to 'give his life as a ransom for many';[3] and that the Son of man, when he came 'in the glory of his Father with the holy angels', would be ashamed of any who, here on earth, had been ashamed of him or of his words.[4] He even claimed and accepted divine prerogatives, for he professed to forgive sins[5] and he received men's worship.[6]

It is not surprising, then, to find that he consistently claimed a unique relationship with God.[7] It is significant that the Synoptic tradition has preserved the Aramaic word *Abba* by which, it would seem, he habitually addressed God; and Paul retained the same Aramaic word 'quite gratuitously embedded in the alien texture of a Greek letter'[8] to emphasize that when we, who are not sons of God by nature, are adopted into his family 'through faith in Christ Jesus',[9] we find that the Spirit of the one, eternal Son makes us address God in the same confident, intimate way.[1] 'This was a child's word; and it seems to have been used in ordinary family life, but never (so far as our information goes) in direct address to God, except on the lips, first of Jesus, and then of Christians; and even Christians soon reverted to the standardized Jewish form "our Father in heaven" . . . It looks, then, as though it was Jesus himself who first dared to use this very simple, family address in his prayer to God. It is one of the three or four Aramaic words and phrases used in the traditions of the words of Jesus. But it is still more striking when St. Paul uses the same Aramaic word to describe what it is that the Holy Spirit

---

[9] Jn. 8:58.    [1] Mk. 2:28.    [2] Lk. 19:10.
[3] Mk. 10:45; Mt. 20:28.    [4] Mk. 8:38. *Cf.* Lk. 12:8.
[5] Mt. 2:2-7; Mk. 9:2-6; Lk. 5:20-24; 7:48.
[6] Mt. 28:9, 17; *cf.* Mt. 4:10.
[7] A. M. Ramsey, *God, Christ and the World*, pp. 86f.
[8] Moule, *op. cit.*, p. 48.    [9] Gal. 3:26.    [1] Rom. 8:15; Gal. 4:6.

enables the Greek-speaking Christians to say.' And it is clear
from the two passages in which Paul depicts Christians as
using this mode of address that our 'ability to cry this cry of
deepest intimacy and of absolute obedience arises from the
presence of the Spirit of God in us as the Spirit of his own Son.
It is therefore a derived sonship – an adoption.'[2]

This unique relationship with God claimed by the Jesus of
the Synoptic tradition is still more clearly emphasized in the
Fourth Gospel. 'For God so loved the world that he gave his
only Son,'[3] he is reported to have said (if we follow Archbishop Temple in believing that the Evangelist was at this
point still recording the words of Christ rather than his own
meditation on their implications). 'My Father has never yet
ceased his work, and I am working too,' he said on another
occasion; and the Evangelist comments, 'This made the Jews
still more determined to kill him, because he was not only
breaking the Sabbath, but, by calling God his own Father,
he claimed equality with God.'[4] And when one of his disciples
came to him and said, in effect, 'Lord, you have often spoken
to us of a heavenly Father. Now just show us the Father, and
that will be quite enough,' he replied: 'Have I been with you
so long, and yet you do not know me? He who has seen me has
seen the Father.'[5] On yet another occasion he quietly remarked, 'I and the Father are one.'[6]

It is true that in this context we must also consider the
apparent contradiction inherent in that cry of dereliction from
the cross, 'My God, my God, why hast thou forsaken me?'
but I should prefer to reserve this for the next chapter. It is
also true that it has often been suggested that he never really
made these claims; instead, they were attributed to him by the
devotion of disciples prone to hagiography. But this will not
do; for whatever view a critic may take of some individual
statement which he is recorded to have made, this quiet
assumption of a unique relationship with God, and the
resultant authority with which he spoke, is one of the ir-
reducible minima of the Gospel story. How else are we to
explain the rage of the Jewish leaders, the accusations of
blasphemy, and the attempts to stone him? To this hostility,

[2] Moule, *op. cit.*, pp. 48–52.               [3] Jn. 3:16.
[4] Jn. 5:17, 18, NEB.          [5] Jn. 14:8, 9.          [6] Jn. 10:30.

and to those accusations that he sought to 'make himself God', not only the New Testament but even the Talmud bears testimony. And it is well to recognize that if these claims were not true he must have been either a megalomaniac or a deceiver – certainly not the most perfect man, and the greatest of all religious teachers, that he has so often been said to be. 'The authority that Jesus claims presupposes a nearness to God, a solidarity with him, that no other man has. What Jesus does is blasphemy unless it springs from special authority. He claims this authority for himself. . . .'[7] And C. S. Lewis writes: 'The historical difficulty of giving for the life, sayings and influence of Jesus any explanation that is not harder than the Christian explanation, is very great. The discrepancy between the depth and sanity and (let me add) *shrewdness* of His moral teaching and the rampant megalomania which must lie behind His theological teaching unless He is indeed God, has never been satisfactorily got over. Hence the non-Christian hypotheses succeed one another with the restless fertility of bewilderment.'[8]

The portrayal of Christ in both the Gospels and the *kerygma* is, moreover, consistently linked with Old Testament prophecies, and to these we must now turn. It is true that critics have professed to find the very basis and explanation of the Gospel records and the apostolic witness in those Old Testament predictions which the primitive church felt that the Messiah must fulfil. But this would make a whole series of factual statements, recorded during the lifetime of eyewitnesses, into deliberate fabrications; and this is a hypothesis which I should find it impossible to reconcile with the ethical teaching of the apostles and their immediate followers and the testimony even of their enemies to the quality of their lives. So I am convinced that the apostolic church came to realize that the person and life of Christ fulfilled predictions which they – like their Jewish contemporaries – had previously been unable to understand.

We will pass over the indirect testimony of the Old Testament in hints of a plurality of persons within the unity of the divine Essence, in 'theophanies' in which 'the angel of the

[7] P. Althaus, as quoted in W. Pannenberg, *Jesus – God and Man*, p. 54.
[8] *Miracles* (Fontana, 1960), p. 113.

Lord' seems to be virtually identified with the God he was
sent to represent, and in the personification of the divine
Wisdom, and concern ourselves exclusively with the direct
prophecies of the one to whom the Jewish nation looked
forward with such ardent longing. But even the most cursory
study reveals that these go far beyond mere predictions of a
conquering King and a suffering Servant – difficult though
the Jews found it to realize that the Messiah would fulfil both
these apparently contradictory strands in Old Testament
prophecy; for there are many indications that the Messiah
would be more than a mere man. His sway was to be universal,[9] endless,[1] utterly righteous[2] and even divine;[3] it would
secure judgment, salvation, deliverance and redemption for
his subjects, while the needy, the afflicted and the friendless
would be his special concern.[4] He is described by the psalmist
as 'my Lord',[5] who sits as eternal priest at God's right hand.[6]
Even kings would come and worship him.[7] He would bear
the sins of others[8] and his death would be the condition of his
victory.[9] Micah speaks of his eternal pre-existence;[1] Jeremiah
describes him as 'The Lord our righteousness';[2] and Isaiah
as 'the Redeemer, the Lord of Hosts',[3] who is also the everlasting Father and the mighty God.[4] These predictions are
the more remarkable in the light of the rigid monotheism which
characterizes the Old Testament revelation of God. But this
summary represents only a fraction of the relevant predictions
and Dr H. P. Liddon can justly speak of 'those successive
predictions of a Messiah personally distinct from Jehovah,
yet also the Saviour of men, the Lord and Ruler of all, the
Judge of the nations, Almighty, Everlasting. . . . One whom
prophecy designates as God'.[5] That the Jewish leaders who
hounded Jesus to his death so totally failed to understand
these prophecies explains why the risen Christ had to open
his disciples' eyes and 'interpreted to them in all the scriptures
the things concerning himself';[6] and it is the fact that he did

[9] Ps. 2:8, 9.                         [1] Ps. 45:6; Is. 9:7; cf. Dn. 7:14.
[2] Je. 23:5; Is. 11:4, 5.             [3] Ps. 45:6.            [4] Ps. 72.
[5] Ps. 110:1.                         [6] Ps. 110:4.           [7] Is. 49:7.
[8] Is. 53:3, 4, 12.                   [9] Is. 53:11, 12.       [1] Mi. 5:2.
[2] Je. 23:6.                          [3] Is. 44:6.            [4] Is. 9:6.
[5] *The Divinity of our Lord*, p. 96.          [6] Lk. 24:27.

so which accounts for the phenomenon that the primitive church seems to have collected together, from the very first, a number of these Old Testament prophecies and used them as part of its catechetical teaching.

Finally, we must ask ourselves how all this was interpreted and applied by the apostolic church, and what its implications are for us today. They are, I think, many and varied.

There has been much talk of late about our 'image' of God; indeed, the quest for God has absorbed the hearts and minds of men and women all down the centuries. How do we visualize him? Do we think of him as a mere principle or force, impersonal and all-pervasive – or, indeed, as the mere 'ground of our being'? The Bible teaches us that God is much more than that: he knows, he wills, he loves; he is holy, just and good; he is emphatically a person. Or is our picture of him basically anthropomorphic – almost like an idealized Father Christmas? The Bible certainly uses anthropomorphic imagery, and speaks of God as seated on his throne, looking down from heaven, stretching out his hand, making bare his arm, *etc.* But God is in fact spirit, and has no body.

How, then, are we to picture him? The Old Testament sternly forbade the use of any image or representation even of the true God. Instead, men were to visualize him in one of the names by which he revealed his nature. But names are a cold comfort for those whose love makes them long to know him and see him in a much more personal way. And Paul echoes the Old Testament when he writes of God as 'the blessed and only Sovereign, the King of kings and Lord of lords, who alone has immortality and dwells in unapproachable light, whom no man has seen or can see. To him be honour and eternal dominion'.[7] So is the quest for something more personal and satisfying doomed to perpetual disappointment? Are we never, even in the life beyond the grave, to *see* God?

It is precisely at this point that the incarnation meets our deepest need. 'No one has ever seen God' was the testimony of John as much as of Paul, but he immediately adds: 'God's only Son, he who is nearest to the Father's heart, he has made him known.'[8] Here the Greek word for 'made known' contains

[7] 1 Tim. 6:15, 16.          [8] Jn. 1:18, NEB.

the root found in 'exegesis', as Professor Blaiklock observes
'Jesus Christ', he says, 'was God's "explanation" of himself,
his "apologia", his "exegesis".'[9] What, then, is our image of
God? Not the uncertain and distorted likeness which the
mystic seeks in his own heart, but the one who uniquely bore
'the very stamp of his nature'[1] and was 'the visible expression
of the invisible God'.[2] It is in the face of Jesus Christ alone that
we can now see the glory of God[3] in an intimate, personal
and satisfying way. And even in the eternal world, as it would
seem, the glory of the Godhead will be made visible – and
bearable to created eyes – only in a glorified Man, who still
bears in some undefinable way the symbols of his passion.[4]

This necessarily means that he is on a par by himself. We
can, of course, compare his teaching with that of Confucius
or Plato; we can compare his miracles with those worked by
the apostles in his name; and we can try to assess the influence
he has exercised down the ages in comparison with that
wielded by others. But just as on the mount of transfiguration
the divine voice forbade any attempt to put Moses and Elijah,
the great law-giver and the representative of the prophets, on a
par with him, and proclaimed him unique in both his person
and authority, so now he utterly transcends all others. Men
can, of course, reject him, to their eternal loss; but to those
who accept the apostolic witness he is the final arbiter.

There are many, however, who would accept this statement
in regard to the glorified Christ, but who would regard it as
inapplicable to the Jesus of the Gospels. Did not the incarnation, they would argue, necessarily involve a laying aside of
his divine knowledge? Does not the apostolic witness itself
speak of him as 'humbling' or 'emptying' himself?[5] Surely,
then, we cannot take all that he said when on earth as divinely
authoritative, for he could then speak only in terms of his age
and environment? Such, in brief, is what is termed the kenotic
theory.[6]

[9] *Layman's Answer*, p. 104.
[1] Heb. 1:3.                          [2] Col. 1:15, J. B. Phillips' translation.
[3] 2 Cor. 4:6.                        [4] Rev. 5:6.
[5] Phil. 2:7. But this has been translated in NEB 'made himself nothing'
(*cf.* AV, 'made himself of no reputation') which probably represents the
basic thought – and may be an echo of Is. 53:12.
[6] The term is derived from the Greek word *kenōsis* ('emptying').

It has, however, been pertinently remarked that this theory, if consistently applied, would involve something very different from the Christian doctrine of the incarnation. On this theory the one who had previously been God emptied himself of his Godhead and became man, only to resume his Godhead after the ascension.[7] But the Bible teaches that he became man without ceasing to be God, and that he has now taken his glorified manhood back into the Godhead. What, then, does this imply as to the authority of all that he said?

At this point we come face to face with the mystery of the incarnation, and how – in theological terms – a divine nature and a human nature could co-exist in one Person. But I think that a significant parallel can be found here between the moral and the intellectual. In the realm of morality the Bible clearly teaches that God as God cannot even be tempted by sin; that man as man is not only tempted but frequently falls into evil; but that God incarnate was tempted (because he had become man) but never sinned (presumably because he remained God). So the parallel in the realm of knowledge would run as follows: God as God is omniscient, and knows all things; man as man is both limited in his knowledge and actually falls into error; but God incarnate was not omniscient (because he had become man), but was never in error (because he remained God). If this is true we can accept all that he said, even on earth, as divinely authoritative.

It will, perhaps, have been noted that I have put no emphasis on the virgin birth in the course of this chapter. This is not because I do not believe in it, for I do; but because, as I understand it, the account of Christ's miraculous birth was given in the Gospels for the sake of those who had already come to believe in him and who wished to know the facts, but was never used as a means of evoking faith in those who were not yet convinced on other grounds as to who he was.[8] After all, a virgin birth would be possible without any implications of deity.[9] But the fact remains that there is a

[7] *Cf.* D. M. Baillie, *God was in Christ* (Faber, 1947), pp. 94ff.
[8] It does not seem to have formed part of the apostolic *kerygma* or proclamation, the very basis of which was the resurrection.
[9] Muslims, for example, believe that Christ was miraculously born of a virgin, but that this display of God's creative power does not mean that Christ was in any way divine.

singular congruity and significance in the miraculous birth, directly from God, of one who utterly transcended mere humanity in so many other ways and whose relationship with God was unique through and through.

It is common today to speak of him as 'the man for others'. Such, indeed, he was; but in a very special way. C. S. Lewis has vividly described the difference between the son whom a man begets and the work of art which he creates. The latter, however fine, is distinct and different from the one who made it, while the former partakes of his very life and nature. Such is the difference between Christ and ourselves. We are created beings – mortal, finite, sinful. He alone was and is, in his very being, the 'only-begotten' Son of God. But through him, and in him, we too can be brought to the experience of sonship; for we can become sons of God by what the Bible variously describes as 'adoption' and 'new birth'. He took our human nature that he might share with us his divine nature.[1]

Because he took our nature, with its limitations and temptations, he is now able to understand, sympathize and save; and if he has in fact implanted in us his nature, we shall not always be as we are now, but shall be transformed one day into his likeness. Then we shall be sons of God in the full meaning of that term.

[1] 2 Pet. 1:4.

# 3 THE ROMAN GIBBET: WAS IT INEVITABLE?

In our consideration of the central figure which dominates the New Testament we have hitherto paid little attention either to his death or alleged resurrection, since each of these was to be the subject of a special study. But an examination of the evidence for the resurrection as physical fact rather than beautiful myth is an essential component in any discussion of the historical basis for the Christian faith or of the view we must take of Christ himself. In regard to the crucifixion, on the other hand, the major question which confronts us is different. Here we are not primarily concerned with its historicity, but its explanation; not so much with whether it happened, but why it happened. As Otto Betz puts it: 'The fundamental fact to which the quest of the historical Jesus always brings us back is his death on the cross. Nowadays the liberal scholar is sometimes reproached with having no adequate explanation for this fact. How could the devout and lovable teacher of a higher morality possibly have been crucified? But has the Bultmann school a better explanation? Why should a prophet and rabbi, a 'voice before the end', be more deserving of the cross than the liberal teacher of a higher ethic? It is not enough to point to Jesus' conflict with the Pharisees and the sovereign manner in which he dealt with the Law ... For no Jewish heretic ever died on the cross.'[1]

Now of the fact that Jesus was crucified there would seem to be virtually no room for denial or debate. To doubt this would be to question the historicity of Jesus himself and of everything that concerns him; and we have already noted the

[1] *What do we know about Jesus?*, p. 83.

overwhelming evidence against such an attitude. All our
sources state that he was 'crucified under Pontius Pilate';
and it is significant that this is asserted with equal insistence
by pagans, Jews and Christians. In the case of the Jews it
would certainly be possible to argue that they would have had
no objection to attributing to Jesus the reprobation of God
as well as man which would be implicit for them in asserting
that he died on a gibbet, since they could then apply to him
the Old Testament declaration that 'cursed is everyone who is
hanged on a tree'.[2] But to Roman writers a reference to the
crucifixion would have been no more than the recording of a
fact of purely secular history. And for Christians falsely to have
attributed such a shameful death to their Lord and Master
would be nothing short of incredible.

From the climate of thought which prevails today it is
easy to underestimate this point. The cross has become such a
symbol of heroic self-sacrifice, and such a focal point of religious devotion, that it is difficult to realize how it must have
appeared at the time of the early church. The closest modern
parallel would be a gallows and a hangman's noose. There was
nothing either romantic or mystical about crucifixion in the
Roman Empire. It was an all too common form of execution,
which not only provided a sickening sight of human agony,
but also a rude reminder of the rule of an alien power. To
die such a death would seem to show that the condemned
man was a failure, a criminal, an object of pity or shame,
repudiated by both God and men. No wonder the apostle
Paul says that the preaching of the cross was to the Jews
a scandal and to the Greeks an absurdity.[3] What possible
motive could there have been for the primitive church to
invent such an end to what they certainly believed was a
life of matchless quality and supreme significance, or to
accept the form of a cross as the central symbol of their faith
and devotion?

Let us take it as certain, then, that Jesus was crucified. But is
it equally certain that he actually died on the cross? It has not
infrequently been argued that he did not. This theory was
first propounded, so far as I know, by Venturini at the end of
the eighteenth century. According to this view Jesus was

[2] Gal. 3:13, NEB.                    [3] 1 Cor. 1:23.

certainly nailed to the cross, but he did not really die. What happened was that pain and loss of blood caused him to swoon and appear to be dead. Do not the Gospels themselves record that Pilate was surprised that he was 'dead already'?[4] Medical knowledge was not very advanced at that time; so he was taken down from the cross and laid in the tomb in the mistaken belief that life was extinct. Then the cool restfulness of Joseph's sepulchre so far revived him that he was eventually able to emerge from the grave; but his ignorant disciples could not accept this as a mere resuscitation, and proclaimed it as a resurrection from the dead.

Such is the theory in bare outline. It has been elaborated in recent years by a heretical sect of Muslims called the Ahmadiya, who assert that the resuscitated Jesus first spent some time in interviews with his disciples in Jerusalem and Galilee; then headed northwards and met the apostle Paul when the latter was travelling from Jerusalem to Damascus; went on as far as north India to take his message to the 'lost sheep of the house of Israel' in the form of a tribe called the 'Beni Isra'il'; and finally died and was buried in Srinagar in Kashmir, where the tomb of an unknown Sheikh is identified as his burial place. None of this is supported by any historical evidence whatever; but it is proclaimed not only as a matter of faith but of almost demonstrable fact. And another variation of Venturini's theory has recently been adopted in a strange book called *The Passover Plot*.[5]

The first objection to Venturini's original suggestion, or its subsequent development by the Ahmadiya, is that the Fourth Gospel[6] is emphatic that steps were taken to make certain that Jesus was dead; for that, surely, must have been the reason for the spear-thrust in his side. But even if, for argument's sake, it is postulated that his life *might* not have been wholly extinct, is it really likely that to lie for hours in a rock-hewn tomb in Jerusalem at Easter, when it can be distinctly cold at night, would so far have revived him, instead of proving the inevitable end to his flickering life, that he would have been able to loose himself from yards of grave clothes weighted by

[4] Mk. 15:44.
[5] Hugh J. Schonfield, *The Passover Plot* (Hutchinson, 1965; Corgi, 1967).
[6] Jn. 19:33ff.

pounds of spices, roll away a stone which three women felt incapable of tackling,[7] and then walk miles on wounded feet?

But it was the sceptic, D. F. Strauss, who, as it seems to me, finally exploded this theory when he wrote: 'It is impossible that a being who had stolen half dead out of the sepulchre, who crept about weak and ill, wanting medical treatment, who required bandaging, strengthening and indulgence . . . could have given the disciples the impression that he was a Conqueror over death and the grave, the Prince of Life, an impression which lay at the bottom of their future ministry. Such a resuscitation . . . could by no possibility have changed their sorrow into enthusiasm, have elevated their reverence into worship.'[8] Nor could the disciples ever have made such a mistake unless Christ himself had deliberately exploited their credulity.

The new slant given to this theory in *The Passover Plot* is equally unconvincing. Dr Schonfield is correct, in my opinion, when he insists that the Jesus of the Gospels is explicable only on the basis that he was profoundly convinced that he was the promised Messiah, and that he understood his Messiahship in terms of the suffering Servant of the later chapters of Isaiah. But Dr Schonfield then goes so far as to suggest that Jesus decided that he must stage what would appear to be a sacrificial death in accordance with Old Testament predictions, although he hoped he might in fact survive. So he carefully concealed this plan from the apostles, and revealed it only to Nicodemus and one or two unknown friends in Jerusalem; he deliberately provoked Judas into betraying him; he arranged for one of those whom I suppose we must call his fellow-conspirators to be ready near the cross with a spongeful of some narcotic to dull his pain and induce unconsciousness; and he planned that Nicodemus and his friends should then take his seemingly lifeless body and nurse it back to health and strength. In the event, however, this plan was thwarted by the spear-thrust in his side. All the same, Dr Schonfield surmises that he may have been revived for a very short time, during which he asked that certain messages might be given to the apostles, before he finally succumbed

[7] Mk. 16:1–3.
[8] *New Life of Jesus* (Williams and Norgate, 1865), Vol. I, p. 412.

and was quietly buried. But none of this was known to the apostles, who sincerely believed that he had died on the cross; and they then, we are asked to believe, mistook the unknown person who tried to bring them Jesus' dying message – or, conceivably, a series of different persons – for the Master they had known so well, and fell into the error of thinking that he had risen from the dead. This seemed to them confirmed by the fact that the tomb was empty.

This is ingenious to a degree. But the book is marked throughout by a willingness to stress the merest detail in the Gospel records where this assists the writer's strange hypothesis, and to reject everything, however important, which points the other way. The possibility that the central figure might have been more than a mere man is not regarded as even worthy of consideration. Instead, he is made to act in such a way as to be guilty of leading those who were the chief recipients of his teaching sadly astray. Nor is there any suggestion as to why the unknown messenger was mistaken for Jesus himself, why the conspirators never told the apostles what had really happened, or what, indeed, would have been the outcome of this fantastic plot if it had succeeded.

None of these suggestions is at all convincing, and there seems to be no doubt whatever that Jesus did in fact die on the cross. But why is it that the New Testament writers appear to have regarded it as inevitable that he should die a criminal's death? Can this be adequately explained in terms of the impact that his teaching and actions might be expected to have had on the Jewish and Roman authorities, and the reactions they were likely to provoke? Why was it that both Sadducees and Pharisees seem to have joined in an unnatural alliance to destroy him, and that the Procurator acceded – most unwillingly, it seems – to their demands?

On the basis of the picture of Jesus drawn by many Liberal Protestant writers it is certainly difficult to understand why the Sanhedrin should have gone so far as to condemn him to death. The ethical ideals represented by the Sermon on the Mount might well provoke ridicule and even opposition, but would scarcely suggest that the one who taught them was so dangerous that he must be destroyed. It is true that he had challenged a form of religion which was largely concerned

C

with the outward and ritual, and had taught that it was the inward attitude of the heart which really mattered; that he had often disregarded the 'traditions of the elders' and even denounced them as contrary to the Scriptures which they claimed to amplify; and that he had repeatedly pricked the bubble of Jewish exclusiveness. These things were enough to explain fierce hostility; but they would not adequately account for this strange combination of both Sadducees and Pharisees in demanding nothing less than his execution.

An examination of the New Testament records reveals that a number of different charges were brought against him at his trial. But basic to them all seems to have been the accusation that he had claimed to be the Messiah. On this point we can certainly agree with Dr Schonfield; and it is easy to see how a claim to be the Messiah, as that term was then interpreted by the Jewish leaders, would naturally be represented as a claim to be a King when he was arraigned before the Roman Procurator. It was such a charge alone which would have overcome the strong repugnance which Pilate seems to have had to condemn him to death; for a claim to be another King would constitute a direct challenge to the Emperor. As Otto Betz puts it: 'it is clear from the very fact of crucifixion that Jesus was executed as a political insurgent according to Roman law. In the inscription on the cross the verdict is explicit: Jesus of Nazareth was "the King of the Jews". Since the Roman emperor had to be acknowledged as the lord of Judaea, a "King of the Jews" was bound to be condemned as a rebel (or "robber") and crucified. There can be no doubt that here the Gospel account is giving the unvarnished historical facts. For what stamps Jesus as a common criminal according to Roman justice cannot be ascribed to any apologetic or dogmatic viewpoint, particularly if Mark wrote his Gospel in Rome.'[9]

This would also explain the decision of the Sadducees that he must be destroyed, for they were primarily concerned with maintaining the political integrity of their nation and with safeguarding their own position. But it is much more difficult, at first sight, to understand why this should have provoked the Pharisees, who made up the greater part of the

[9] *What do we know about Jesus?*, p. 84.

Sanhedrin, to an equally insistent demand for his death. This can, I think, be explained only by the further charge that he was guilty of blasphemy – a charge which would make the death penalty appropriate under Jewish law. And this, in its turn, means that he must have claimed to be more than Messiah, as that term was then understood by the Jewish leaders.

Let me quote from a recent essay by Professor C. H. Dodd: 'The evangelists, I conclude, John and the Synoptics alike, take the view that Jesus was charged with blasphemy because he spoke and acted in ways which implied that he stood in a special relation with God, so that his words carried divine authority and his actions were instinct with divine power. Unless this could be believed, the implied claim was an affront to the deepest religious sentiments of his people, a profanation of sanctities; and this, I suggest, is what the charge of "blasphemy" really stands for, rather than any definable statutory offence. . . . Whether or not Jesus had put himself forward as Messiah, the implied claim was messianic at least, perhaps rather messianic plus.'[1]

But for the New Testament writers to regard condemnation on such a charge as inevitable, need (in theory, at least) mean no more than that they were convinced that one who made such claims could expect only a martyr's death. The evidence is overwhelming, however, that they believed that his death was voluntary and that no man could have killed him against his will. 'For this reason the Father loves me,' he is recorded to have said (little though they understood him at the time), 'because I lay down my life, that I may take it again. No one takes it from me, but I lay it down of my own accord. I have power to lay it down, and I have power to take it again; this charge I have received from my Father.'[2] This is echoed in the Synoptic tradition that in the Garden of Gethsemane he forbade his disciples to try to protect him, with the words, 'Do you think that I cannot appeal to my Father, and he will at once send me more than twelve legions of angels? But how then should the scriptures be fulfilled, that it must be so?'[3]

[1] 'The Historical Problem of the Death of Jesus', in C. H. Dodd, *More New Testament Studies* (Manchester University Press, 1968).
[2] Jn. 10:17, 18.                    [3] Mt. 26:53, 54.

It is obvious, then, that they regarded the crucifixion as something more than a martyr's death, inflicted on its victim against his will. On the contrary, the early church clearly believed that the inevitability of the cross came from the will and purpose of Jesus himself, as well as Jewish malignity and Roman connivance. He had taught that men should love even their enemies; that they should not resist those who sought to do them harm; that they should be willing to 'lose' their lives in order to 'save' them. But everyone knows that example is much more potent and persuasive than precept, and that actions speak louder than words. It was in a sense inevitable, therefore, that he should not only live as an example to others, but also die as their supreme example. 'Greater love has no man than this,' he himself said, 'that a man lay down his life for his friends.'[4] Nor did this example go unheeded, for the apostles subsequently taught that 'Christ also suffered for you, leaving you an example, that you should follow in his steps',[5] and that 'It is by this that we know what love is: that Christ laid down his life for us. And we in our turn are bound to lay down our lives for our brothers'.[6]

All this is perfectly true so far as it goes, but it does not go nearly far enough. In their understanding of the meaning of the cross men are seldom in error in what they assert, but often in what they deny. It is true that it was almost inevitable, on a purely human level, that Jesus would meet a martyr's death; and it is also true that he no doubt felt compelled to go willingly to such a death as an example to mankind. But the New Testament writers do not attribute the inevitability of the cross exclusively to the machinations of his enemies or to the desire of Jesus himself to put his ethics into practice. On the contrary, the teaching of the early church gives a primary emphasis to what I shall call the Godward rather than the manward aspect of the cross. Nor do they hesitate for a moment to combine the two: the moral responsibility of those who compassed his death, and the divine purpose which lay behind their evil deed. 'This Jesus,' Peter is recorded as saying on the Day of Pentecost, 'delivered up according to the definite plan and foreknowledge of God, you crucified and

[4] Jn. 15:13.   [5] I Pet. 2:21.   [6] I Jn. 3:16, NEB.

killed by the hands of lawless men.'[7] And it is equally certain
that they depicted Jesus himself as voluntarily going to his
death for a much more fundamental purpose than to provide a
living – or dying – example of his ethical teaching.

If we are to take the Gospels at all seriously, it is inescapable
that Jesus himself regarded the cross as inevitable not primarily because of the hostility of the Jewish leaders, nor because
he wanted to set a supreme example of self-sacrificing love
and patient endurance, but because this was his Father's will
and an essential part of his mission. Dr Schonfield is indubitably right, as we have seen, when he insists that the Jesus of
the Gospels was utterly convinced not only that he was the
Messiah, but also that this must be interpreted primarily
in terms of the suffering Servant of the later chapters in
Isaiah. Dr Vincent Taylor, in three consecutive books on the
atonement, has come to precisely the same conclusion, and
has emphasized the supreme place occupied by Isaiah 53
in the way in which Jesus himself interpreted his mission.

One of the most striking features in the Gospel records is the
divine imperative which seems continually to have prompted
Jesus' words and actions. Right from the time when, at the age
of twelve, we read that he gently rebuked Mary and Joseph
with the words 'Did you not know that I must be about my
Father's business?'[8] this divine imperative seems to have
dominated his life. 'I must give the good news of the kingdom
of God to the other towns also, for that is what I was sent to
do,'[9] he said early in his ministry. And as soon as Peter confessed, at Caesarea Philippi, that he was the Christ, he
began to teach his incredulous and unwilling disciples that
'the Son of man must suffer'.[1] With increasing frequency,
moreover, we find this divine imperative identified with, and
based on, the fulfilment of the Old Testament scriptures.
'The Son of Man is going the way appointed for him in the
scriptures'[2] was one way in which he referred to what he knew
lay before him; and he went on: 'You will all fall from your
faith; for it stands written: "I will strike the shepherd down
and the sheep will be scattered".'[3] It is abundantly clear that

[7] Acts 2:23. *Cf.* A. M. Ramsey, *God, Christ and the World*, p. 89.
[8] Lk. 2:49.         [9] Lk. 4:43, NEB.
[1] Mk. 8:31.         [2] Mk. 14:21, NEB.         [3] Mk. 14:27, NEB.

his life was lived, more and more, under the shadow of the cross. 'The scripture *must* be fulfilled,' he said on a number of different occasions; and on the very road to Gethsemane he quoted from Isaiah 53 and said: 'For I tell you that this scripture must be fulfilled in me, "And he was reckoned with transgressors".'[4] So it is not surprising that the risen Christ summed it all up by asking: 'Was it not necessary that the Christ should suffer . . .?'[5]

But why, we may ask, was the cross so inevitable from the point of view, not of men, but of God? To this several different answers have been given – all of them correct in their fundamental assertions, however misleading they may be in their denials or implications. This is particularly true of the answer we shall consider first, which may be termed the subjective view of the atonement. Commonly associated with Abelard (AD 1079–1142), a younger contemporary of Anselm of Canterbury, it explains the atonement in terms of a change which is effected in man rather than in God. Abelard's major emphasis was that the cross represents the supreme demonstration of God's love to sinful men. Naturally enough, this attitude was welcomed by many theologians of the 'Enlightenment' in the last two centuries, and was sometimes given extravagant expression. But it is best understood, I think, if we summarize it in a way which is as close as possible to the teaching of the New Testament.

By nature we all love our own way; so we rebel against God and hate his demands on our lives and consciences. As a result, there exists what can be described only as a state of enmity, conscious or unconscious, between us and God, and we stand in desperate need of what the New Testament calls 'reconciliation'. But the Greek word for reconciliation not only conveys the sense of making peace and bringing together persons who were previously alienated from each other, but also of a change of heart which is effected in one or both of them. Who, then, the argument goes, needed this change of heart? Here both reason and the New Testament seem to answer that this was primarily true of men rather than God. 'God is love', we read; 'God so loved the world'; 'in this is love, not that we loved God but that he loved us.'[6] It is

[4] Lk. 22:37.      [5] Lk. 24:26.      [6] I Jn. 4:8; Jn. 3:16; I Jn. 4:10.

man who rebels and hates; so it is man whose attitude needs
to be changed. And this seems to be the primary sense in which
the New Testament speaks of reconciliation. 'For if while we
were enemies', wrote Paul to the Romans, 'we were reconciled
to God by the death of his Son, much more, now that we are
reconciled, shall we be saved by his life.'[7] It was at the cross
that God demonstrated or 'commended' his love towards us.[8]
'From first to last this has been the work of God', Paul wrote
to the Corinthians. 'He has reconciled us men to himself
through Christ, and he has enlisted us in this service of reconciliation. What I mean is, that God was in Christ reconcil-
ing the world to himself, no longer holding men's misdeeds
against them, and that he has entrusted us with the message
of reconciliation. We come therefore as Christ's ambassadors.
It is as if God were appealing to you through us: in Christ's
name, we implore you, be reconciled to God!'[9]

We shall note, later, that this is by no means the only side
of the atonement, and clear indications of the other side can
be discerned even in the New Testament use of the term
'reconciliation'. But according to the 'subjective' view the
*primary* emphasis is that men are reconciled to God by a
change of attitude which he effects in them. How, then, does
he do this? The answer is that he does it by and through the
cross. For men, as we have seen, love themselves and their
own way, and hate God and his demands – so they have a very
inadequate view of the meaning and effects of sin. But when
they come to see how evil sin is in the sight of a holy God –
so black that even he could deal with it only at the cross;
and when they realize that the God who must always hate
sin yet infinitely loves the sinner – so much so that he was
willing to go, in the person of Christ, all the way to an agonizing and shameful death; then they experience a change of
heart, and begin to hate themselves and their sin and to 'love
him, because he first loved us'.[1]

Now all this is perfectly true, and it is, indeed, an important
aspect of the atonement. It is quite unnecessary to distort
this emphasis by remarking, as Dr Rashdall does of Abelard,
that 'he sees that God can only be supposed to forgive by
making the sinner better, and thereby removing any demand

[7] Rom. 5:10.  [8] Rom. 5:8, AV.  [9] 2 Cor. 5:18-20, NEB.  [1] I Jn. 4:19, AV.

for punishment'.[2] As Abelard himself put it: 'To us it appears
that we are none the less justified in the blood of Christ and
reconciled to God by His singular grace exhibited to us in that
His Son took our nature, and in it took upon Himself to
instruct us alike by word and example even unto death, (and
so) bound us to Himself by love; so that, kindled by so great a
benefit of divine grace, charity should not be afraid to endure
anything for His sake.'[3] In other words, as he states elsewhere,
it is man's grief for sin which makes him 'fit to be saved'.
Such a distortion of New Testament teaching would accord
well enough with the paramount emphasis put today on the
reformative motive in punishment; but the basic idea in the
subjective interpretation of the cross may more worthily
be expressed by saying that God is always longing to forgive
and that the problem he had to solve is how to make man
*receive* his forgiveness, since true forgiveness necessarily implies
a new relation between two or more persons. According to
this view the fundamental meaning of the atonement is that
God, our loving heavenly Father, always suffers when his
children sin, but we are too hardened and rebellious to
believe this or to let it affect our attitude and conduct. So he
came in the person of his Son to die a death which constituted
the supreme demonstration of his love, thus making clear
in time and human history what had always been true in the
eternal and transcendent world. It is only when we come to
understand this, even dimly, that our rebellion is silenced
and our pride is abased; and we are ready, at last, humbly to
accept the forgiveness which God has always been waiting
to bestow.

As we have seen, this view has a firm basis in the New
Testament itself. Every time we sing that well-loved hymn
'When I survey the wondrous cross' we are giving expression
to it;[4] for the emphasis, throughout the whole hymn, is on the
subjective effect which a contemplation of the love and suffering of the cross effects in our cold and selfish hearts. But it
does not at all follow from this that the meaning of the cross
is exclusively subjective and that there was no objective

[2] *The Idea of Atonement in Christian Theology* (Macmillan Lord, 1919), p. 359.
[3] Quoted by H. Rashdall, *ibid.*, p. 359.
[4] *Cf.* L. Morris, *Glory in the Cross* (Hodder and Stoughton, 1967), p. 61.

necessity for it which is at least equally – or even more – fundamental. On the contrary, the biblical evidence for an interpretation of the atonement which is not confined to its effect on the hearts of men and women, but which involves a radical transformation in the situation in which they find themselves – a transformation which could be accomplished in no other way – seems to me overwhelming.

When we try to determine in what, precisely, this objective necessity for the cross consists we again find ourselves faced with a division of opinion – or at least of emphasis – between what Gustaf Aulén terms the 'dramatic' or 'classical' view of the atonement, on the one hand, and the 'juridical' or 'Latin' view, on the other.[5] The first of these finds considerable support in the early Fathers, quite apart from the New Testament; while the second is usually traced back to Anselm of Canterbury, although it, too, has a firm basis in the Bible. Both interpretations have at times been grossly exaggerated, and even caricatured; but both, in essence, express truths without which no interpretation of the atonement would be adequate.

The 'classical' view sees the meaning of the cross chiefly in a victory which God himself won in Christ over hostile powers – Satan, sin, death and hell. Some of the early Fathers took this idea to the most extravagant lengths. They argued not only that men by their sin had come under the power of Satan, but that he had acquired rights over them; and they did not hesitate to assert that when Jesus said that he had come to 'give his life a ransom for many', that ransom was paid to Satan to set his captives free. Some of them even pictured God as making a bargain with Satan, offering to let him have Christ if he would release the souls of believers. But then, as Dr Leon Morris puts it, 'Satan found that he had over-reached himself. He could get Christ down to hell when the Father handed him over, but he could not keep him there. On the first Easter Day Christ rose triumphant. He burst the bonds of hell and broke free. He returned to heaven whence he came and Satan was left lamenting. He had lost the souls he gave up in exchange for Christ, and he had lost Christ too.'

Nor were the Fathers who propounded this view in the least disconcerted by the fact that this transaction with Satan looks suspiciously like trickery and deception. On the contrary, they gloried in the fact that God 'could out-scheme Satan as well as defeat him in a test of strength. One of the greatest of the early theologians, Gregory of Nyssa, likened the process of salvation to a fishing expedition. The deity of Christ was the fish-hook and his flesh the bait. Satan took the bait and was destroyed like any poor fish. And even Augustine of Hippo, surely one of the profoundest intellects of all time, improved on this only by substituting a mouse-trap for a fish-hook!'[6]

But the extravagance of such views should not obscure the fact that the New Testament itself declares that at the cross a victory was in fact won over Satan and the powers of darkness. It was by his death, the writer of the Epistle to the Hebrews asserts, that Christ destroyed 'him who has the power of death, that is, the devil' and delivered 'those who through fear of death were subject to lifelong bondage'.[7] And it was at the cross, Paul says, that Christ 'disarmed the principalities and powers and made a public example of them, triumphing over them'.[8] There is no need to press the imagery to the extent of asking to whom the ransom price was paid, and the New Testament never does this. But the fact remains that the victory was won, that Satan's captives were set free, that sin was 'put away' and that death and hell were vanquished. If God is God, and if God is love, it was essential that this victory should be won; and it could be won only at the cross. Hence the inevitability of the Roman gibbet. But Christ did die and rise again, and Paul could exclaim, 'O Death, where is your victory? O Death, where is your sting? The sting of death is sin, and sin gains its power from the law; but, God be praised, he gives us the victory through our Lord Jesus Christ.'[9] It is this aspect of the cross, as Aulén reminds us, which has always inspired the triumphant exultation of our Easter hymns.

The chief reason why this view does not greatly appeal to the modern mind is not so much the crude imagery in which some of the Fathers depicted it, as the fact that many today question the existence of a personal devil and regard any idea of

[6] *Glory in the Cross*, pp. 65f. *Cf.* G. Aulén, *op. cit.*, pp. 63ff.
[7] Heb. 2:14, 15.    [8] Col. 2:15.    [9] 1 Cor. 15:55–57, NEB.

God winning a victory over hell, death and sin as involving a form of dualism. But it seems inescapable that while 'the absolute Dualism between Good and Evil typical of the Zoroastrian and Manichaean teaching, in which Evil is treated as an external principle opposed to God', must be rejected, yet there is a genuine opposition 'between God and that which in His own created world resists His will; between the Divine Love and the rebellion of created wills against Him'.[1]

We noticed in passing, in chapter 2, how the Fourth Gospel speaks of Christ being not merely grieved but positively angry or 'enraged' at the tomb of Lazarus; and this anger was not caused by his sisters' failure in faith or the unrestrained wailing of their guests, but rather by the ugly phenomenon of death itself. For death – or at any rate death as we now know it – would have had no place in a perfect world. On the contrary, death as corruption and decay, and hell as the epitome of spiritual death, are both the result of rebellion and sin; and the God who loves the sinner necessarily hates both sin and its foul results. 'The spectacle of the distress of Mary and her companions enraged Jesus', in the words of B. B. Warfield, 'because it brought poignantly home to his consciousness the evil of death, its unnaturalness, its "violent tyranny" as Calvin phrases it. In Mary's grief he contemplates – still to adopt Calvin's words – "the general misery of the whole human race" and burns with rage against the oppressor of men.'[2] Nor is this divine antipathy lessened by the fact that both death and hell are judgments passed by God himself on the sin of which they are the necessary outcome.

This apparent ambivalence is vividly illustrated by the attitude of Martin Luther[3] – and, indeed, of a number of passages in the New Testament – to the 'Law'. It was God's law, and therefore essentially 'holy and just and good'; yet the apostle could write that 'sin gains its power from the law',[4] and that 'those who rely on obedience to the law are under a curse'.[5] So man had to be 'discharged from the law'[6] and

[1] G. Aulén, op. cit., p. 20.
[2] The Person and Work of Christ (Presbyterian and Reformed Publishing Co., 1950), pp. 116f.
[3] Cf. G. Aulén, op. cit., pp. 67, 82ff.     [4] 1 Cor. 15:56, NEB.
[5] Gal. 3:10, NEB.                            [6] Rom. 7:6.

'redeemed . . . from the curse of the law'[7] in the sense of a way of legal righteousness which he could never attain and which even provoked the very sins it forbade.[8] So regarded, the law was itself one of the enemies from which Christ delivered us.

The First Epistle of John echoes this emphasis on a victory over hostile powers when it asserts that 'the reason the Son of God appeared was to destroy the works of the devil',[9] to 'take away sins',[1] and that we might pass 'out of death into life'.[2] This is why both the incarnation and the cross were inevitable. But it is noteworthy that the New Testament teaching about the cross as our 'ransom' and means of redemption puts a primary emphasis on the fact that Christ's death was *instead* of ours, that he paid our debt and took our place, and that what he did was therefore not only vicarious but substitutionary in its significance.[3]

What Aulén calls the juridical or Latin view, on the other hand, finds the primary necessity for the atonement in the character of God himself. God is infinitely loving, but he is also holy and just; and the infinitude of his love for the sinner is itself the measure of his antipathy to the sin which constitutes an inevitable barrier between the sinner and himself. This is expressed in the New Testament in terms of the righteous judgment of God on sin and his 'wrath' against it – a wrath which is utterly different from the petulance which so often characterizes human anger, and which, far from being inconsistent with his love, is in fact its obverse side. Sin, the Bible teaches, is 'sinful beyond measure';[4] and the God who is himself the moral order of the universe cannot ignore it or act as though it did not exist. He longs to forgive the sinner, but this can be done only on a moral basis. First, sin must be shown in its real light, judged and punished; only then can forgiveness be glad and free.

It will be objected by some, no doubt, that this is to go back to the retributive theory of punishment rather than to concentrate – as many advocate today – exclusively on its re-

[7] Gal. 3:13.          [8] *Cf.* Rom. 7:7–11.          [9] 1 Jn. 3:8.
[1] 1 Jn. 3:5.          [2] 1 Jn. 3:14.
[3] Mk. 10:45. See also Gal. 3:13 and 2 Cor. 5:21. The word 'substitutionary' is a technical term meaning that Christ so took our place as to bear the guilt and penalty of sin as our 'substitute'.          [4] Rom. 7:13.

formative and deterrent purposes. But this represents a shallow and inadequate attitude to the whole problem of crime and penology. To reform criminals, if this can be done, and to restore happiness and equilibrium to those whose crimes can often be traced to inward frustration, misery and despair, are obviously of fundamental importance; and we have already seen how the cross, when properly understood, is uniquely able to transform hostility into love, pride into humility, and indifference into devotion. Nor would anyone deny the importance of the deterrent element in punishment. But both the reformative and deterrent purposes in punishment would lack any adequate moral basis were there not also a retributive element involved – the conviction that the criminal *deserves* such treatment, that his crime merits it, and that there is a necessary connection between the degree of his guilt and the severity of the penalty he must bear. If we concentrate on the reformative purpose alone, the criminal who is already sorry for what he has done should never be punished at all, however heinous his crime, and the criminal who is so hardened as to be beyond reformation should equally escape any penalty whatever. If, on the other hand, we stress the deterrent element alone, then severe punishment might often be imposed for a comparatively trivial misdeed, while all penalties should properly be discarded as utterly useless in some of those major crimes in which they are most unlikely to have the necessary effect. But this would outrage the moral conscience. Even in everyday life it would be dangerous in the extreme to allow would-be reformers to take whatever action they believed to be best calculated to effect the necessary change in a social misfit, or to give unfettered reign to the motive of deterrence, without the essential moral basis that men and women must not be treated contrary to their deserts or to fundamental considerations of justice. The trouble is that it is impossible for a human judge to know all the relevant facts – heredity, environment, temperament, circumstances and temptation – on which any completely just assessment of guilt must be based. But none of these considerations applies to God. He knows everything, and he can and does judge with absolute justice and understanding. But on that basis which of us could ever lift up our heads?

The problem, then, is obvious. God is love, and he longs to reconcile and forgive the sinner. But God is also 'light', or absolute moral holiness, and he cannot ignore the fact of sin. Sin must be judged, expiated, punished. There was only one way in which this problem – and the resulting tension, if we may so speak, in the very character and nature of God – could be resolved. God himself came in the person of his Son to live in the world he had made and to experience the frustrations and temptations inherent in human nature; and God in Christ identified himself with our sin and bore its penalty and consequences. So now he can be seen to be just and righteous, and to have vindicated the moral order, when he pardons and justifies the repentant sinner.

It is, of course, as easy to caricature this view of the inevitability of the cross as we saw to be true of the 'dramatic' or classical view. It has in fact often been so caricatured, not only by its opponents but by those who most passionately proclaim it. Not infrequently it has been represented in terms of a stern and angry God being placated by a kind and loving Christ; or in terms of God visiting the sins of the guilty on the only *man* who was 'good enough to pay the price of sin'. Both perversions of the doctrine must be repudiated. The New Testament teaching about the 'propitiation' – for that is the word which, above all others, sums up what we are now trying to understand – does not carry the idea of sinful men seeking to appease a vengeful deity. On the contrary, the New Testament asserts that 'Herein is love' – love at its very highest and best – 'not that we loved God, but that he loved us, and sent his Son to be the propitiation for our sins'.[5] It was not we who provided the propitiation, but he; and it was his incomparable love for the sinner which prompted him to do it. It was not Christ, apart from God, who provided it; it was God in Christ who planned and accomplished it. But the propitiation was necessary, none the less.

Inevitably, this can be described as a juridical view. The Bible speaks repeatedly of God as the judge of men, of sin as not only breaking our fellowship with him but deserving his righteous judgment and condemnation, and of the wonder of his grace in 'justifying' – or declaring 'not guilty' – the

[5] 1 Jn. 4:10, AV.

repentant sinner. But the juridical aspect, though inescapable, must not be exaggerated. The idea, so prominent in the Middle Ages, that the cross completed a juridical 'satisfaction' for sin which the sinner could not adequately make for himself, is a dangerous perversion. This view, in its extreme form, insisted on man undergoing penances for his sins and trying to atone for them by works of supererogation, but emphasized that neither the one nor the other could ever 'satisfy' a holy God. So God himself, in Christ, provided an all-sufficient penance for sin, and an incomparable life of undeviating obedience, which made up for every human deficiency.

But the teaching of the Bible is far more radical than this. Any picture of the Day of Judgment which depicts it in terms of a giant pair of scales, with our sins on one side and our good deeds on the other and with the righteousness of Christ thrown into the balance in our favour, is utterly erroneous. The Bible teaches that a single sin is enough to separate us from God.[6] Our salvation can never be in any measure from ourselves. It is the work of God alone, who by his free, unmerited favour declares sinners to be 'not guilty', free of the law, because he has himself, in the person of Christ, taken our place when he 'bore our sings in his own body on the tree',[7] So sin is not only forgiven but forgotten.

The question is often asked whether Christ took our place as our representative or as our substitute. The answer must surely be that he was both. It seems to me that this is not only clearly taught by the language of the New Testament, but is also necessarily inherent in the fact that Christ was both God and man. As man he could never be our substitute; that would be grossly unjust. The prophet Ezekiel taught, long ago, that no man could ever bear another's sin or guilt.[8] Similarly, as God he could never, by definition, be our representative. It is only because Christ was both God and man that we find in his atoning death both a substitutionary and a representative element.

It is important to emphasize, in this context, that the New Testament teaching about 'reconciliation' itself clearly includes something which has been done by God to alter the position on his side as well as on man's side. It was not, of course, that

[6] Jas. 2:10.        [7] 1 Pet. 2:24.        [8] Ezk. 18:4, 20.

he had to change from hatred to love, for unlike man he was always loving. But his 'wrath' against sin, which D. M. Baillie defines as 'identical with the consuming fire of inexorable divine love in relation to our sins', had to be averted by the propitiation which he provided when in Christ he reconciled the world to himself. As H. Maldwyn Hughes puts it: 'What the Atonement achieves is a change in the relation of persons, and no such change can be brought to pass without both parties being affected. Reconciliation is necessarily twofold . . . when God reconciles us to Himself, our relation to Him, and His relation to us are both set on a new basis.'[9] From God's side the fundamental change was that sin had now been judged and punished, so forgiveness could be glad and free. This is clear from the fact that Paul bases his entreaty to us to be reconciled to God on the fact that God had made Christ 'to be sin' for us and no longer held our misdeeds against us;[1] and that he speaks about us having received (or 'been granted'[2]) the reconciliation. As P. T. Forsyth insists: 'Reconciliation was finished in Christ's death. Paul did not preach a gradual reconciliation. He preached what the old divines used to call the finished work . . . He preached something done once for all – a reconciliation which is the base of every soul's reconcilement, not an invitation only.'[3]

The church has always been of one mind in asserting that the cross is at the very heart of its faith and message, but there have been many different views, as we have seen, as to *how* it saves men from sin. One reason for this, as Dr Morris says, is the complexity of the subject. 'Sin can be regarded from many aspects. It is at one and the same time a transgressing of God's law, a debt, an incurring of guilt, a coming under the power of evil, and much more. Obviously anything that is able to deal effectively with all the aspects of all the sins of all men will itself be exceedingly complex. We must not expect it to be so simple that a child can understand it all. And when a thing is necessarily complex there is bound to be a certain amount of disagreement as to what it means essen-

[9] *What is the Atonement?* (James Clarke, 1924), pp. 20f., quoted in L. Morris, *The Apostolic Preaching of the Cross* (Tyndale Press, 1965 edition), p. 248.
[1] 2 Cor. 5:19, 21.          [2] Rom. 5:11, NEB.
[3] *The Work of Christ* (Fontana, 1965), p. 90.

tially.'[4] Properly viewed, however, the different ways in which the utter necessity for the cross has been explained are not contradictory but complementary. It is not a question of choosing one of these views to the exclusion of the others, but of seeing how the full truth necessarily includes them all.

The subjective view, as we have seen, is profoundly true, provided it is not taken in isolation. Man does, indeed, need a radical change of heart; he needs to begin to hate his sin instead of loving it, and to love God instead of hating him; he needs, in a word, to be reconciled to God. And the place, above all others, where this change takes place is at the foot of the cross, when he apprehends something of the hatred of God for sin and his indescribable love for the sinner. But the cross would not really have demonstrated God's hatred of sin had there been no need, on God's side, for the propitiation which alone makes it possible for him to forgive the sinner. Far from detracting from the cross as a demonstration of God's love, this gives it a validity and profundity it would otherwise lack. What would be the point of an empty display of love by a death which was utterly unnecessary except for its subjective appeal? It would be like a man saying that he would throw himself into the sea and give his life to demonstrate the depth of his affection for someone standing safely on a pier. This might be love, but it would savour of lunacy. How different it would be, however, if he had plunged into the water to rescue a drowning man, and had succeeded in saving him at the cost of his own life. That would be true love – love in action – rather than empty sentiment. So the love of God was demonstrated at the cross not by an empty show, but by his saving men from judgment and condemnation in the only way in which this could be done. And it was shown not primarily by the physical agony of crucifixion, but by the infinite spiritual cost of bearing the sin of the world.

Much the same line of argument also applies to the 'dramatic' or 'classical' view. It is certainly true that God won the victory at the cross over Satan, sin, death and hell, and that he set their captives free. But this was done not only by Christ 'tasting death for every man', but by his being 'made sin' for us and becoming the propitiation for our sins. And the basic

[4] *Glory in the Cross*, pp. 58f.

need for this propitiation could be only in the character of God himself.

How else can one explain the words of Isaiah 53, that 'he was wounded for our transgressions, he was bruised for our iniquities; upon him was the chastisement that made us whole, and with his stripes we are healed. All we like sheep have gone astray; we have turned every one to his own way; and the Lord has laid on him the iniquity of us all'?[5] How else can one understand the sacrificial system, and John the Baptist's identification of Christ as 'the Lamb of God, who takes away the sin of the world'?[6] How else can one explain Christ's own statement that 'this is my blood of the new covenant, which is poured out for many for the forgiveness of sins'?[7] How can one understand the agony in Gethsemane, except in terms of a ghastly shrinking, not primarily from the physical pain of crucifixion, but from bearing the world's sin? Or the awful cry of dereliction from the cross, except in terms of an agonizing experience of that severance of relationship with God which is the basic and inevitable consequence of sin? Of course we cannot explain *how* the Son who was eternally of one substance with the Father could experience this. That would be to plumb the innermost mystery of the Godhead, which is not given to mortal men. But that does not alter the revealed fact that this is what happened, and that he was in fact 'made sin' in our place. As Dr Campbell Morgan puts it: 'The logical, irresistible, irrevocable issue of sin is to be God-forsaken. Sin in its genesis was rebellion against God. Sin in its harvest is to be God-abandoned. Man sinned when he dethroned God and enthroned himself. He reaps the utter harvest of his sin when he has lost God altogether. That is the issue of all sin. It is the final penalty of sin, penalty not in the sense of a blow inflicted on the sinner by God, but in the sense of a result following upon sin, from which God Himself cannot save the sinner. Sin is alienation from God by choice. Hell is the utter realisation of that chosen alienation. Sin therefore at last is the consciousness of the lack of God, and that God-forsaken condition is the penalty of the sin which forsakes God. Now listen solemnly, and from that Cross hear the cry, "My God, My God, why hast Thou forsaken Me?"

[5] Is. 53:5, 6.          [6] Jn. 1:29.          [7] Mt. 26:28.

THE ROMAN GIBBET: WAS IT INEVITABLE? 83

That is hell . . . On that Cross He was made sin, and therein He passed to the uttermost limit of sin's outworking.'[8]

It is clear, then, that no examination of Christianity as a historical religion can fail to give the cross a central place. But this in itself is not enough; for we need to reckon not only with the fact that Christ died, but with the reasons why the Bible and the church join in asserting that this was both necessary and inevitable. That theologians should differ as to why, precisely, this was so, is scarcely surprising. The great fact on which the New Testament insists, Dr Morris remarks, 'is that the atonement is many-sided and therefore completely adequate for every need. Do we appear as guilty sinners deserving death? Our death penalty has been borne. Are we enslaved to sin? The price has been paid and we are redeemed. Are we unable to realize the greatness of the love of God? The cross reveals it as nothing else can. Do we need an example to show us which way to go? Christ gives us that example in His death.'[9]

So we might go on. 'However we understand man's plight, the New Testament sees the cross as God's complete answer. Whatever needed to be done to put away our sin and to make us safe for eternity He has done. The atoning work is satisfying and complete.'[1] That is the explanation of the triumphant cry which echoes down the ages from that tortured figure on a Roman gibbet: 'It is finished!'[2]

[8] *The Crises of the Christ* (Pickering and Inglis, 1945), pp. 215f.
[9] *Glory in the Cross*, pp. 8of.    [1] *Ibid.*    [2] Jn. 19:30.

# 4 THE EMPTY TOMB: WHAT REALLY HAPPENED?

In this last chapter we come, inexorably and inevitably, to consider what really happened on the first Easter morning. For the belief that Christ rose from the dead is not an optional extra of Christian theology, superimposed on his life and death to give a happy ending to what might otherwise be regarded as a tragedy of infinite beauty overshadowed by doubts as to whether it was not, after all, a supreme example of magnificent defeat. On the contrary, it is the linchpin of each one of our previous studies.

In the first chapter, 'The historical basis: is it convincing?', we saw that one of our very earliest and best-attested pieces of evidence for the *kerygma* of the primitive church is the terse statement in 1 Corinthians 15 – almost credal in its form – that the apostolic tradition, at the very inception of the Christian faith, was 'that Christ died for our sins, in accordance with the scriptures; that he was buried; (and) that he was raised to life on the third day, according to the scriptures'[1] – together with the assurance that this was not a tradition peculiar to Paul, but one shared and proclaimed by all the apostles.[2] It is significant, moreover, that Paul not only argues that, if Christ was not risen, then both his preaching and his readers' faith were without foundation, but also that the apostles themselves must be regarded as 'lying witnesses for God'[3] – for their assertion of the fact of the resurrection had not been based on any *a priori* conviction that the Messiah must necessarily rise again, nor on any subjective assurance that he had in fact done so, but rather on a number of incidents in which one and another of them, or whole companies

[1] 1 Cor. 15:3, 4, NEB.    [2] 1 Cor. 15:11.    [3] 1 Cor. 15:15, NEB.

of them together, testified that they had actually seen the risen Christ and conversed with him. These possibly 'mystical' experiences were, moreover, brought right down to earth by their conviction that the tomb was empty and that Christ's mutilated human body had not only disappeared but been transformed into a different sort of body. To this point we shall return later.

It seems, therefore, that the credibility of the whole apostolic testimony must stand or fall according to the view we take of the resurrection. We shall, of course, have to consider the possibility that they were so mesmerized by a series of hallucinations, or psychological experiences of some sort, that they not only became convinced of their Master's spiritual survival, but were driven to interpret this in terms of a resurrection from the dead. It is precisely at this point that it will become imperative to assess the evidence for the allegation that the tomb was empty, and to consider whether this could, in any case, be explained on any rationalistic basis.

Of one thing we can be sure: namely, that the proclamation of the resurrection lay at the heart of the apostolic preaching from the very first. The triumphant faith and witness of the first generation of Christians (as evidenced by all the New Testament documents and even – however indirectly – by pagan and Jewish testimony, to say nothing of the over- whelming circumstantial evidence provided by the growth of the primitive church) is inexplicable except on the basis of their conviction that the one whom they had come to accept as the promised Messiah, only to see their hopes wither into despair before the tragedy of the crucifixion, had in fact triumphed over death and the grave. But this, too, will demand more detailed consideration.

The conclusion to which we come with regard to the re- surrection is equally relevant – indeed, fundamental – to the subject of our second chapter, 'The central figure: how are we to regard him?' It is clear that Paul considered the resurrection to be the supreme proof of the deity of Christ, for he wrote that he was 'declared Son of God by a mighty act in that he rose from the dead'.[4] It was, moreover, a personal confronta- tion with the risen Christ which evoked from Thomas the

[4] Rom. 1:4, NEB.

doubter the first full confession of Christian faith when he exclaimed 'My Lord and my God!'[5] and which prompted the apostles as a whole to give him the worship which belongs to God alone. But why, it may be asked, should this be so? After all, other risings from the dead are recorded in both the Old and New Testaments, yet no-one has suggested that the persons so raised were in any sense divine.

To this two answers may be given. The first is that the resurrection of Christ is clearly distinguished, in the biblical records, from all those instances of men and women who were called back from death and the grave to a renewal of physical life, and who inevitably had to die again later. The resurrection body of Christ, Paul asserted in 1 Corinthians 15, was not a 'natural' body but a 'spiritual' body, whatever that may mean; and elsewhere he unequivocally declared that the risen Christ would never die again, but that death no longer had 'dominion over him'.[6]

But even a resurrection of this sort would not be beyond the power of an omnipotent God. After all, it is to such a resurrection that we all look forward one day. So the true answer to the question why the resurrection was regarded by the early church – and should be regarded by us today – as the final proof of the deity of Christ, must be found in the nature of the claims which he made during his life and ministry. As we saw in chapter 2, it is recorded that on a number of different occasions he foretold that he would not only be crucified but would rise again on the third day; and this, as Frank Morison powerfully argues,[7] is the inescapable interpretation of his enigmatic declaration 'Destroy this temple, and in three days I will raise it up'[8] – a declaration which formed an important element in the accusations brought against him at his trial before the Sanhedrin.[9] He even promised his bewildered disciples that after he had risen from the dead he would go before them into Galilee.[1] So it is clear that, if nothing had happened after their sad farewell to him on the cross or in the tomb, they (and certainly subsequent generations) would have concluded on reflection that he must have

[5] Jn. 20:28.                    [6] Rom. 6:9.
[7] *Who Moved the Stone?* (Faber, 1930).
[8] Jn. 2:19.        [9] Mt. 26:61; Mk. 14:58.        [1] Mt. 26:32.

been mistaken and that his predictions could not be relied upon.

But even a foreknowledge and prediction that he would die and rise again, and a vindication of this prediction by its literal fulfilment, would not necessarily prove his deity. Some of his recorded assertions, however, went a good deal further than this. He claimed on one occasion, as we have seen, not merely that God would raise him from the dead but that he himself had power to lay down his life, and power to take it again – and even that this power of his was, in some sense, the reason for his Father's love.[2] And on another occasion he asserted that he was himself both the resurrection and the life.[3]

But the point at issue is even more fundamental than this. As we saw in chapter 2, he frequently made claims which would have sounded outrageous and blasphemous to Jewish ears even from the lips of the greatest of prophets. He said that he was in existence before Abraham and that he was 'lord' of the sabbath; he claimed to forgive sins; he continually identified himself, in his work, his person and his glory, with the one he termed his heavenly Father; he accepted men's worship; and he said that he was to be the judge of men at the last day, and that their eternal destiny would depend on their attitude to him. Then he died. It seems inescapable, therefore, that his resurrection must be interpreted as God's decisive vindication of these claims, while the alternative – the finality of the cross – would necessarily have implied the repudiation of his presumptuous and even blasphemous assertions.

Very similar considerations apply also to the subject of our third chapter, 'The Roman gibbet: was it inevitable?' Without the resurrection the natural interpretation of the cross would be a martyr's death, whether imposed upon him against his will by the malignity of his enemies or welcomed by him as the supreme opportunity to put his ethical teaching into practice. It might, I suppose, still be regarded as a demonstration of the love of God, except that this demonstration, in itself, seems to depend on the unique relationship of the one who died to the God whose love he was demonstrating. But the so-called 'classical' view of the victory of the cross would be meaningless on such a basis, for the shout of victory over

[2] Jn. 10:17, 18.　　　　[3] Jn. 11:25.

Satan, sin, death and hell which rings through the New
Testament and our Easter hymns is always associated with
the dual message of Good Friday and Easter Day, with the
cross *and* the resurrection, and would be empty and hollow
if the Roman gibbet had not been followed by the empty
tomb. And even on the more juridical view of the meaning of
the atonement, it is the resurrection which vindicates the
efficacy of what Christ did on the cross. How else could we
know that his sacrifice was accepted, that his death was
indeed our ransom and that his blood was in fact the means
and guarantee of the remission of our sins? It was with this
thought in mind that Paul declared that Christ 'was put to
death for our trespasses and raised for our justification'[4] –
using the term 'justification' not in the sense in which he
usually employs it (namely, of the means by which sinful men
and women are accounted or accepted as righteous in the
sight of a holy God), but rather in the sense in which we find
it used in James 2 (namely, as the evidence and proof of
that acceptance).

So the assertion of the primitive church that Christ did in
fact rise from the dead is absolutely crucial to our whole
subject, from beginning to end. Even Professor W. Pannenberg, who considers the Gospel records of the life and teaching
of Jesus as, in part, a projection into the past of the church's
experience of the resurrection, regards the evidence for the
resurrection itself as so convincing that he makes it the foundation stone of his whole thesis.[5] It is particularly noteworthy in
this connection, moreover, that he is totally unimpressed by
the argument which maintains that the *kerygma* of 1 Corinthians 15 is concerned only with the resurrection appearances,
but knows nothing of an empty tomb – and that this was a
later addition found exclusively in the Gospels. Whatever a
Greek might have thought about a mere spiritual survival,
he maintains, it would have been impossible for a Jew of the
first century to write of Christ having died, having been
buried and having been 'raised to life' if he thought of his
body as still rotting in the tomb.[6] And what would have been

---

[4] Rom. 4:25.          [5] *Jesus – God and Man*, pp. 108, 66ff., *etc.*
[6] *Ibid.*, pp. 74ff. He made this point much more clearly in a talk I had with
him in Harvard University in January 1967.

the point in adding the words 'on the third day' if he was thinking of no more than a spiritual survival?

It is totally inadequate to suggest, with Bultmann, that the resurrection is not an event which evidence attests, but rather a mythological way of proclaiming the saving significance of the cross – and that all the historian can affirm is the Easter faith of the disciples.[7] On the contrary, the resurrection, as Dr A. M. Ramsey insists, is 'something which "happened" a few days after the death of Jesus. The apostles became convinced that Jesus was alive and that God had raised him to life. It is not historically scientific to say only that the apostles came to realize the divine meaning of the Crucifixion for them or that the person of Jesus now became contagious to them. Something *happened* so as to vindicate for them the meaning of the Cross, and to make the person of Jesus contagious to them. The evidence for a stupendous happening, which the New Testament writers mention, was the survival of the Church, the appearances of Jesus in a visible and audible impact on the apostles, and the discovery that the tomb was empty. The several elements in this threefold evidence no doubt had different degrees of evidential weight for different people, and they have such varying degrees still.' The resurrection faith was certainly, in one aspect, evidential. 'But, *pace* Bultmann, there was another side to the process of belief. The apostles, for all the existential character of the Easter faith, were yet at pains to confirm to themselves and to others that it was a reasonable faith and that there were facts inexplicable apart from the Resurrection. There was not only the challenge of the existential encounter: there was also the challenge of evidence, the challenge to explain a number of events and experiences other than by the Resurrection. . . . To value these evidential factors is not, as Bultmann suggests, to lapse into a worldly-minded historicism, for the Easter faith, existential as it is, was and is related to evidential history. Christians believe in the Resurrection partly because a series of facts are unaccountable without it.'[8]

Let us now examine the evidence for the resurrection, therefore, more in the manner of the lawyer than that of the

[7] A. M. Ramsey, *God, Christ and the World*, p. 52.
[8] *Ibid.*, pp. 78–80.

theologian. It rests, in the first place, on the unequivocal
testimony of Paul to which reference has already been made;
and it is significant that he includes in the list of resurrection
appearances, which he appends to his summary of the apostolic tradition, one occasion on which the risen Christ appeared to more than five hundred persons at once, and that he
remarks that the majority of these witnesses were still alive
when he wrote.[9] He also refers to the resurrection repeatedly
in one after another of his letters; and he positively affirms
that this was the message of the other apostles too.[1] This is
confirmed by the three Synoptic Gospels – in accounts which,
it is obvious, are largely independent of each other – and by
John's Gospel; it represents the heart and thrust of Peter's
sermons as recorded in the Acts of the Apostles; and it is the
very basis of the ascription of praise to God the Father with
which the First Epistle of Peter begins. It has already been
remarked, moreover, that Paul tells us that his testimony in
1 Corinthians 15 represents the tradition which was passed
on to him – probably by Ananias immediately after his
conversion, and certainly by Peter and James on the occasion
of his visit to Jerusalem in about AD 35 or very soon after;
so there can be no reasonable doubt whatever that it goes
right back to the first decade of the Christian era.[2]

How, then, can the fact of the resurrection be denied? The
most radical alternative – that the stories of Easter and the
succeeding forty days were mere lies or fabrications – must
be decisively repudiated. Think of the number of the witnesses;
of the quality of the ethical teaching which they gave to the
world and which, even on the testimony of their enemies,
they lived out in their lives; of the fact that none of them, even
under the pressure of sustained persecution or a martyr's
death, ever went back on the testimony he had given. Consider, too, the psychological absurdity of suggesting that a
band of men should almost overnight be transformed from
craven cowards huddled in an upper room into a company of
witnesses whom no opposition could silence, by nothing
more convincing than a miserable deception which they
conspired to foist upon the world. That would not make sense.

The idea that these stories might have been legends rather

[9] 1 Cor. 15:6.          [1] 1 Cor. 15:11.          [2] See chapter 1, pp. 27f.

than lies seems at first sight somewhat more plausible. Had it been possible to date the records a century or two after the event – and repeated attempts to do precisely this have been made by a series of brilliant scholars – the suggestion might have been feasible. But the attempt has decisively failed, crushed under a weight of contrary evidence; and there can be no reasonable doubt that the testimony to the resurrection can be traced back to the very first decade after the event. It seems meaningless, therefore, to speak of legends when we are dealing, not with stories handed down from generation to generation, but accounts given by the eyewitnesses themselves or attributed to them while they were still present to confirm or deny them. Besides, who can read these stories with any care and then dismiss them as mere legends? It would have been a great temptation to a legend-monger to recount some story of how the resurrection happened; yet no such attempt finds a place in the New Testament. What legend-monger would ascribe the first interview with the risen Christ to Mary Magdalene, a woman of no great standing in the Christian church? Would he not have ascribed such an honour to Peter, the leading apostle; or to John, the 'disciple whom Jesus loved'; or – more likely still, perhaps – to Mary the mother of our Lord? And who can read the story of the appearance to Mary Magdalene, or the incident in which the risen Christ appeared to two disciples on an afternoon walk to Emmaus, or the episode in which Peter and John raced each other to the tomb, and seriously conclude that these are legends? They are far too dignified and restrained; far too true to life and psychology. The difference between them and the sort of stories recorded in the apocryphal gospels of a century or two later is both striking and significant.

No; so far as I know, no critic today suggests that these stories are either lies or mere legends.[3] On the contrary, all admit – as admit they must – that the apostles firmly believed that their Master had 'risen from the dead'; but they then proceed to suggest that this belief was a subjective conviction rather than one based on any adequate objective evidence. All the attempts to rationalize the stories of Easter which I have

[3] Although some, of course, believe that there have been legendary accretions to the basic facts.

encountered are characterized, moreover, by the fact that the critics make a clear-cut distinction between the records of the empty tomb on the one hand, and of the resurrection appearances on the other. First the empty tomb is explained away by means of a number of ingenious hypotheses; and then the resurrection appearances are dismissed as some form of hallucination or psychological experience which convinced the apostles but had no objective reality.

First, then, the problem of the empty tomb. The earliest attempt to explain this phenomenon is recorded in Matthew's Gospel, where we are told that the Jewish leaders bribed the guard which had been set to watch the sepulchre to say that the disciples had come by night and stolen the body.[4] But no-one, so far as I know, accepts this story today. It would be incredible both in ethics and psychology. Imagine the apostles raiding the tomb by night, stealing the body, burying it furtively in some other place, and then proceeding to foist this miserable fraud upon the world. This would run totally contrary to all we know of them: their ethical teaching, the quality of their lives, their steadfastness in suffering and persecution. Nor would it begin to explain their dramatic transformation from dejected and dispirited escapists into witnesses whom no opposition could muzzle.

Better than this is the suggestion that the body might have been moved to another grave, for some reason or other, on the orders of the chief priests or the Jewish Procurator, or even of Joseph of Arimathea. But we need to remember that in seven short weeks Jerusalem was seething with the apostles' preaching of the resurrection. They were proclaiming it up and down the city to the great discomfiture of the chief priests, who were being accused of having conspired to crucify 'the Holy and Righteous One'[5] at the hands of an alien power – and were prepared to go to almost any lengths to stamp out this dangerous teaching. Why, then, when the apostles started preaching the resurrection, did they not issue an official denial, and state that the body had been moved on their orders? If this would not have sufficed, they could have called as witnesses those who had carried it away. If this was not

[4] Mt. 28:11-15.          [5] Acts 3:14.

enough, they could have pointed to its final resting-place, or even produced the body itself. They could have exploded this disturbing heresy finally and decisively. Why, then, did they not do so? The answer seems inescapable: because they could not; because they did not themselves know where the body was. And exactly the same argument would apply to the Roman Procurator. The Romans, too, must have been most disturbed by this proclamation that a criminal so recently executed because he claimed to be a King, in apparent rivalry to the Emperor, had risen again from the dead. It is incredible that if the body had been moved on their orders they would not have told the chief priests and taken steps to crush this dangerous movement, at its very beginning, by showing that the apostles' preaching was without foundation.

What, then, of Joseph of Arimathea? The answer is, I think, that the critics cannot have it both ways. They must either accept what the Gospels say, that he was a secret disciple; or they must suppose that he was a pious Jew, who agreed to bury the body in his own tomb so that it might not hang on the cross on the sabbath day. But if he was a Christian it is most unlikely that he would have moved the body without consulting the apostles first; and it is fantastic to suggest that he would not have told them afterwards, when they were preaching the resurrection up and down the city. Yet this would lead to the impossible hypothesis that the apostles themselves were blatant deceivers preaching a miracle which they knew perfectly well had never happened. If, on the other hand, he was just a pious Jew, then it is unlikely that he would have moved the body without asking the permission of the chief priests, and it is incredible that he would not have told them afterwards, when they were so upset by this proclamation of the resurrection. But why, then, did they not annihilate this dangerous heresy at its very inception by issuing an official denial, by calling Joseph as a witness, or even by producing the body itself?

It is true that Dr Schonfield, in *The Passover Plot*, has posed yet a third possibility – namely, that Joseph was indeed a secret disciple, but that he was involved in a curious conspiracy with Jesus himself and one or two others which was kept secret from the apostles. But I will not repeat what I have already said about this book,[6] except to remark that I find it wholly unconvincing and utterly alien to the character of Jesus.

Another attempt to explain the phenomenon of the empty tomb was first advocated, I believe, by Kirsopp Lake. The women who saw where Christ was buried, we are reminded, were strangers in Jerusalem, and their eyes may have been blinded by tears. They went to the tomb, moreover, in the half-light of early morning. They might have missed their way and gone to the wrong tomb. This, he suggests, was precisely what happened; and a young man, who chanced to be hanging around, guessed what they wanted. 'You seek Jesus . . . who was crucified,' he told them. 'He is not here' (pointing to the tomb at which they were looking); 'see the place where they laid him' (pointing to another tomb).[7] But the women became frightened and ran away; and subsequently they decided that the young man must have been an angel who was proclaiming the resurrection of their Master from the dead.

This theory is most ingenious, but it scarcely stands up to investigation. To begin with, it is based on accepting the beginning and the end of what the young man said, but rejecting the most important part in the middle. For what . . . young man is recorded as having said was 'You seek Jesus the who was crucified. *He has risen*; he is not here; see the place where they laid him.' This changes the whole meaning; and it seems a strange thing for a scholar to mutilate the record in this way without any textual authority whatever. Even so, the theory does not seem to make much sense; for if the women had gone straight back to the apostles with this story, they would surely have done one of two things: either they would have gone to the tomb themselves to investigate what had happened, or they would have started to preach the resurrection at once. Yet all the records state that they did not do this for another seven weeks; and no Christian would have had any reason to invent this interval. So we are asked to believe that the women did not, in fact, tell the apostles this story for some weeks, since the latter had all left Jerusalem post haste for Galilee. (No doubt Galilee was a healthier spot for Christians just then, but we are not told why the apostles were so singularly ungallant as to run away and leave all their womenfolk behind – wives, sisters and mothers!) The women, it is suggested, remained alone in Jerusalem, for no apparent reason; and it was only some weeks later, when the apostles came back, already convinced by some psychological experiences that Christ was still alive, that they told them this story – and the apostles then put two and two together and made seven or eight out of them and started preaching the resurrection. But on this hypothesis the body of Christ would still have been lying in Joseph's tomb, about which the chief priests must have known or could so easily have made enquiries. So why did they not obliterate this dangerous movement by denying the very basis of the apostolic preaching, or even by displaying the decomposing body of the one whose resurrection was so confidently proclaimed?

Yet another theory, as we saw in the last chapter,[8] tries to explain the empty tomb by suggesting that Christ did not actually die on the cross at all. Swooning from pain, shock and loss of blood, he was thought to be dead, taken down and laid in the sepulchre. After some hours, however, he revived, and was able to emerge; and his ignorant disciples mistook this resuscitation for a resurrection from the dead. But this theory does not stand up to investigation any better than the others.

Nor would it be any more convincing to suggest that the body might have been stolen by persons wholly unconnected with either the apostles or the chief priests. Quite apart from asking why they should have done this, or remarking on the curious coincidence this would represent, it would seem most unlikely that they would not have confessed what they had done, or have let the truth somehow leak out, when Jerusalem was thrown into such a turmoil by the preaching of the resurrection. The chief priests would have welcomed them with open arms, whatever their guilt, if they could have exploded this most inopportune and inconvenient heresy.

So the empty tomb stands, a veritable rock, as an essential element in the evidence for the resurrection. To suggest that it was not in fact empty at all, as some have done, seems to me ridiculous. It is a matter of history that the apostles from

[8] See pp. 62ff.

the very beginning made many converts in Jerusalem, hostile
as it was, by proclaiming the glad news that Christ had risen
from the grave – and they did it within a short walk from the
sepulchre. Their message 'could not have been maintained in
Jerusalem for a single day, for a single hour, if the emptiness
of the tomb had not been established as a fact for all concerned'.[9] Any one of their hearers could have visited the
tomb and come back again between lunch and whatever may
have been the equivalent of afternoon tea. Is it conceivable,
then, that the apostles would have had this success if the body
of the one they proclaimed as risen Lord was all the time
decomposing in Joseph's tomb? Would a great company of
the priests and many hard-headed Pharisees have been
impressed with the proclamation of a resurrection which was
in fact no resurrection at all, but a mere message of spiritual
survival couched in the misleading terms of a literal rising
from the grave?

It is also noteworthy in this context that all the references
to the empty tomb come in the Gospels, which were written
for Christians who wanted to know the facts. In the public
preaching to those who were not yet convinced, as recorded
in the Acts of the Apostles, there was an insistent emphasis on
the resurrection, but not a single reference to the tomb. For
this I can see only one explanation. There was no point in
speaking of the empty tomb, for everyone – friend and foe
alike – knew that it was empty.[1] The only points worth
arguing about were why it was empty, and what its emptiness
proved.

Yet in point of fact the tomb was not wholly empty. In
one of the most vivid of all the stories about the first Easter
morning we read how Peter and John, summoned by Mary
Magdalene's news of the stone which had been rolled away
from the entrance to the sepulchre, set out to investigate.

[9] P. Althaus, as quoted by W. Pannenberg, *Jesus – God and Man*, p. 100.
[1] W. Pannenberg states that 'the early Jewish polemic against the Christian
message about Jesus' resurrection, traces of which have already been left in
the Gospels, does not offer any suggestion that Jesus' grave had remained
untouched. The Jewish polemic would have had to have every interest in the
preservation of such a report. However, quite to the contrary, it shared the
conviction with its Christian opponents that Jesus' grave was empty. It
limited itself to explaining this fact in its own way . . .' (*ibid.*, p. 101).

Half-way along the road they started to run; and John, the younger man, outran Peter and got there first. Stooping down, he looked in, we read, and saw the grave clothes, but did not go in. Then Peter arrived, characteristically blundered straight in, and took note of 'the linen clothes lying, and the napkin which was on his head, not lying with the linen clothes but apart, wrapped into one place'.[2] Then John too went into the tomb and saw, it seems, how the napkin lay by itself, separated from the other grave clothes by the space where Christ's neck had been, and still wound up – as though the body had been somehow withdrawn, leaving the linen wraps just as they were. This was evidence enough for him, and he needed no more: he 'saw and believed'.

It is also significant that no suggestion has come down to us that the tomb became a place of reverence or pilgrimage in the days of the early church. Even if those who were convinced Christians might have been deflected from visiting the sepulchre by their assurance that their Master had risen from the dead, what of all those who had heard his teaching, and even known the miracle of his healing touch, without joining the Christian community? They, too, it would seem, knew that his body was not there, and must have concluded that a visit to the tomb would be pointless.

When we turn to the resurrection appearances, the basis of our assessment must be rather different. It is manifestly impossible to be dogmatic about the relative roles played by objective and subjective elements in such experiences. One man may see an angel when another does not, but this does not prove that the angel had no objective reality. The one who affirms that he saw him may, indeed, be indulging in fantasy; but it is equally possible to postulate that a certain subjective awareness must be added to objective reality before an angel, who is normally invisible to human eyes, may be seen by men.

All the same, hallucinations and similar phenomena conform, I am told, to certain rules. To begin with, they seem to be confined to persons of certain psychological types. But it is impossible to reduce those who claimed to have seen the risen Christ to any such classification. There was Mary Magdalene,

[2] Jn. 20:6–8, Archbishop Temple's translation.

D

who may have been an emotional and highly-strung young woman. But there was also a hard-headed tax collector, a 'doubting Thomas' and a number of down-to-earth fishermen – together with a heterogeneous crowd of some five hundred persons.

Again, experiences of this kind are highly individualistic, since they spring, in part at least, from the past experiences and subconscious minds of the persons concerned. One man's hallucinations, therefore, will almost certainly differ from another's. But here, we are told, five hundred people on one occasion had the very same 'hallucination' at the same time; while on other occasions ten, eleven, and seven individuals had precisely the same 'fantasy'. So it looks very much as though these experiences were based on objective facts rather than subjective impressions.

Such experiences, moreover, usually concern some expected event. A mother whose son runs away to sea, let us suppose, lights a lamp every evening in the confident hope that he will one day come home; and eventually she imagines that she sees him walking in at the door. But in this case the evidence is convincing that the apostles were not expecting any such thing. They ought to have been, since Christ had foretold his death and resurrection; but they had not begun to understand what he was talking about. Instead, they were despondent, disillusioned and dispirited.

Hallucinations and similar experiences also, I am told, normally occur at suitable times and in appropriate surroundings. But it is impossible to reduce the resurrection appearances to any such formula. There were two near the tomb early on Easter morning; one in the course of an afternoon walk into the country; another, on the same day, in the form of a personal interview, presumably in broad daylight; two or more in a room in the evening; one on a hill in Galilee, and another beside the lake; and yet another on the Mount of Olives.

Finally, hallucinations, if repeated at all, normally go on recurring over a very considerable period – either increasing in frequency until some crisis is reached, or decreasing in frequency until they die away. But in this case five hundred people claim to have had one such experience, and a number of people to have had several such experiences, all during a period of forty days. Then these 'hallucinations' abruptly ceased, and not one of the persons concerned ever claimed to have had another. True, Paul subsequently claimed to have had a vision of the risen Christ when he was on the road to Damascus, and John on the island of Patmos. But it is clear, I think, that these and other visions which people have claimed to have had down the ages – and which, in the case of Paul and John, I unhesitatingly accept as genuine – differed in substance from what happened during the forty days when the risen Christ went in and came out among his disciples in what they afterwards described as 'many infallible proofs'.[3]

Nor is it feasible, in my view, to explain the resurrection appearances in terms of the phenomena claimed by modern spiritism. I am no authority on this subject; but it is impossible to find any one medium present on all occasions, or even the usual group of seekers after the supernatural. And the one who appeared seems to have been very different from alleged spiritist emanations. He could be distinctly heard and clearly seen, even in broad daylight – although his resurrection body was different from his 'natural' body, and he was recognized only with some difficulty. He could withdraw from grave clothes, leaving them, it would seem, still wound up; he could pass through closed doors; he could appear and disappear: yet he could invite a finger to explore the mark of the nails in his hands, or the spear wound in his side. And he could even eat a piece of broiled fish.

But should not this last point, at least, be regarded as a mythological addition to the true facts of the resurrection? Does it not betray a tendency to equate the resurrection with a return to natural life, with its need for food and sustenance? Some would, indeed, have it so. For myself, I am convinced that Christ's deathless spirit returned to his mutilated human body and that this was transformed into what Paul calls a 'spiritual' body.[4] What that is like I frankly do not know;

[3] Acts 1:3, AV. It is true that in 1 Cor. 15 Paul refers to his own encounter with the risen Christ as though it were on a par with the appearances to the other apostles; but he probably means that his experience was as real and 'objective' as theirs, not that theirs was as 'visionary' as his.
[4] 1 Cor. 15:44.

but there is so much else which we do not understand, living
as we do in a world of three dimensions. This transformed
body would certainly not have needed food; but that does not
mean that the risen Christ *could* not have eaten, any more than
that he *could* not be touched. And the reason for his request
for food seems to me clear enough. Had it not been for this,
his disciples might have concluded, once his visible presence
was withdrawn from the upper room, that they had merely
seen a vision. But when they looked at the bones of the fish
and the plate on which it had lain this interpretation of their
experience would be impossible; they had objective proof that
someone had really been there.

But however this may be, it seems to me of fundamental
importance to remember that the empty tomb and the
resurrection appearances go together. It is easy to argue that
all that really signifies is that the Christ of the Gospels is alive
today, and that men can still come to know him. What does
it matter, then, what happened to his body? In reply it must
be emphasized that not only does the credibility of the
apostolic witness stand or fall by the validity of their testimony
on this point, but also that it is the empty tomb which decisively
differentiates between the resurrection of Christ and any sort
of ghost story. It is not merely that Christ is still spiritually
alive and that his disciples somehow became aware of this;
the evidence points to the fact that his wounded body was
transformed, that he left the tomb, that he 'showed himself
alive after his passion by many infallible proofs', that he
ascended to heaven, and that we now have a glorified Man
on the throne of the universe.

In addition, there is evidence of a more general kind. First,
there is the existence of the Christian church. This institution
can be traced back in history to Palestine early in the first
century. But to what did it owe its origin? Its documents of
association, as a lawyer might term them, state unequivocally
that it owed its very inception to the resurrection of its founder
from the dead. This was the fundamental conviction and
message of the apostles and their entourage. 'From the very
first', as Professor Moule has reminded us, 'the conviction that
Jesus had been raised from death has been that by which their
very existence has stood or fallen. There was no other motive

to account for them, to explain them. . . . At no point within the New Testament is there any evidence that the Christians stood for an original philosophy of life or an original ethic. Their sole function is to bear witness to what they claim as an event – the raising of Jesus from among the dead. . . . The one really distinctive thing for which the Christians stood was their declaration that Jesus had been raised from the dead according to God's design, and the consequent estimate of him as in a unique sense Son of God and representative man, and the resulting conception of the way to reconciliation.'[5] It is not too much to say, with C. S. Lewis, that 'The Resurrection, and its consequences, were the "gospel", or good news which the Christians brought: what we call the "gospels", the narratives of Our Lord's life and death, were composed later for the benefit of those who had already accepted the *gospel*. They were in no sense the basis of Christianity: they were written for the converted. The miracle of the Resurrection comes first.'[6]

Again, there is the phenomenon of the Christian Sunday, which can be traced back in history to much the same date and place. But large numbers of the first Christians were Jews, fanatically attached to the Jewish sabbath. It would have taken something of supreme importance to make them change their day of rest and synagogue worship at the end of each week for special meetings on the first day. It did; it took the resurrection. It was to celebrate this that they met, on the same day on which Christ rose, to partake of the meal which symbolized his atoning death.

There is also the festival of Easter, which occupies much the same place in history. But Easter would be utterly meaningless without the death and resurrection which it commemorates.

Then, too, there is that significant interval of seven weeks between the event and its first public proclamation. As has already been observed, no Christian would have invented this. But how can it be explained – except on the basis of the Gospel records, which tell us that the apostles were absorbed, for the first forty days, in intermittent interviews with their risen Lord, and that they then waited a further ten days, on

[5] *The Phenomenon of the New Testament*, pp. 11, 14, 18.
[6] *Miracles*, pp. 147f.

his instructions, until the Holy Spirit came upon them in power?

There is also the striking change which took place in the apostles themselves, to which general references have been made already. How can one explain the change in Peter, from a man who denied his Master three times before household servants to one who told the chief priests to their face that God had raised from the dead the one whom they had crucified, and who then went on: 'there is salvation in no one else, for there is no other name under heaven given among men by which we must be saved'?[7] The New Testament tells us the secret. The broken-hearted Peter, with his self-confidence shattered, had a private interview with his risen Lord;[8] and later the Holy Spirit came upon him.[9] What transformed James, Christ's unbelieving brother throughout the years of his ministry, into the chairman or bishop of the Jerusalem church a few years later? The New Testament reveals this secret too, for we read that the risen Christ had a personal interview with James.[1] This explains why he subsequently wrote about his human brother as 'the Lord of glory'.[2] As W. Pannenberg puts it: 'The Easter appearances are not to be explained from the Easter faith of the disciples, rather, conversely, the Easter faith of the disciples is to be explained from the appearances.'[3] And what of Paul? How can we account for the fact that the arch-persecutor of the Christian church so soon became its greatest missionary – except on the basis of his vision of Christ on the road to Damascus? And is it conceivable that such a man as he would not have checked up on the facts regarding Joseph's tomb, were it not that he must have known already that it was empty? What the vision of the risen Christ showed him in a flash was why the tomb was empty, and who its former occupant really was.

We have already noted, moreover, that Paul not only insisted that Christ 'died for our sins in accordance with the scriptures', but also that he 'was raised on the third day in accordance with the scriptures'.[4] No doubt one of the predictions he had in mind was Psalm 16:9–11, which reads: 'Therefore my heart is glad, and my soul rejoices; my body

[7] Acts 4:12.   [8] Lk. 24:34.   [9] Acts 2:1ff.; 4:8; etc.   [1] I Cor. 15:7.
[2] Jas. 2:1.   [3] Jesus–God and Man, p. 96.   [4] I Cor. 15:3, 4.

THE EMPTY TOMB: WHAT REALLY HAPPENED?

also dwells secure. For thou dost not give me up to Sheol, or let thy godly one see the Pit. Thou dost show me the path of life; in thy presence there is fullness of joy, in thy right hand are pleasures for evermore.'[5] Another passage to which he would almost certainly have pointed is Psalm 110:1; for it is clear that Peter interpreted the words 'The Lord says to my lord: "Sit at my right hand, till I make your enemies your footstool" '[6] in terms of the resurrection. And another possible passage is the prediction in Isaiah 53, just after the most explicit references in the Old Testament to the vicarious nature of Christ's death and to some of the circumstances of his crucifixion and burial, that 'when he makes himself an offering for sin, he shall see his offspring, he shall prolong his days; the will of the Lord shall prosper in his hand; he shall see the fruit of the travail of his soul and be satisfied . . . Therefore I will divide him a portion with the great, and he shall divide the spoil with the strong; because he poured out his soul to death, and was numbered with the transgressors'[7] – a passage which Christ himself asserted, on the very road to Gethsemane, *must* be fulfilled in him. But it is obvious that it was only after Christ had in fact risen from the grave that the early church could have discovered in these Old Testament predictions the import they subsequently saw them to bear.

There is also the fact that Christ himself, as B. B. Warfield puts it, 'deliberately staked his whole claim to the credit of men upon his resurrection. When asked for a sign he pointed to this sign as his single and sufficient credential.'[8] Just as Jonah was a sign to a previous generation, he said, so would his death and subsequent resurrection transcend any and every other proof of who he really was. Now it is obvious, I should have thought, that he could not have meant that this decisive proof would be provided by a purely spiritual survival of physical death and a manifestation of himself to his disciples which would be no more than a ghost-like apparition. He must have been referring to a resurrection of his body from the grave – transformed, no doubt, into a 'spiritual' body. Only so could he be touched, or need to tell people *not* to touch him.[9] And it is precisely at this point that we perceive the

[5] *Cf.* Acts 25–28.    [6] *Cf.* Acts 2:33–36.    [7] Is. 53:10, 11.
[8] *The Person and Work of Christ*, p. 537.    [9] Jn. 20:17.

meaning of the ascension. 'All the accounts suggest', as C. S. Lewis puts it, 'that the appearances of the Risen Body came to an end; some describe an abrupt end six weeks after the death . . . A phantom can just fade away; but an objective entity must go somewhere – something must happen to it. And if the Risen Body were not objective, then all of us (Christian or not) must invent some explanation for the disappearance of the corpse. And all Christians must explain why God sent or permitted a "vision" or "ghost" whose behaviour seems almost exclusively directed to convincing the disciples that it was not a vision or a ghost but a really corporeal being. If it were a vision then it was the most systematically deceptive and lying vision on record. But if it were real, then something happened to it after it ceased to appear. You cannot take away the Ascension without putting something else in its place.'[1]

Then again, there is the testimony of Christian experience down the ages, and the multitude of men and women – rich and poor, learned and ignorant, respectable and reprobate – who have found in the risen Christ their joy, peace and certainty. All down the centuries he has continued to say, 'Here I stand knocking at the door; if anyone hears my voice and opens the door, I will come in and sit down to supper with him and he with me.'[2] He still says the same today. This is not, of course, to suggest that every Christian has a vivid, mystical experience of the risen Lord; but it means that the man who counts on the resurrection, and invites the living Christ into his heart and life as Saviour and Lord, will find his faith confirmed by the inward testimony of the Holy Spirit.[3]

Finally, there is the uniqueness of the one who rose. However natural it might seem for someone to say that, whatever the evidence, he could never believe that Tom Smith could lie for hours in a tomb and then rise from the dead, this would not apply to the central figure of the Gospels. Quite apart from the resurrection, there is excellent evidence, as we saw in chapter 2, that he was much more than a mere man. The incredible thing, to my mind, is that such as he should ever have died 'for us men and for our salvation'. But, granted that he did die, is it really surprising that he should rise again?

[1] *Miracles*, pp. 152f.      [2] Rev. 3:20, NEB.      [3] Rom. 8:16.

Could we not affirm with Peter that it was impossible that death should 'keep him in its grip'?[4]

It is true that the different accounts of the resurrection seem, at first sight, somewhat contradictory in points of detail, although it is by no means impossible to reconcile them.[5] There is a very real sense, however, in which their very discrepancies, real or fancied, strengthen their weight. It is notorious that men and women who give evidence of incidents which they have seen never tell precisely the same story. Inevitably they see the same thing from different angles, and they never take in every detail; they remember some of the facts and forget others; and their stories are complementary rather than identical. If several witnesses tell precisely the same story, any competent judge will recognize at once that they must have been drilled by their lawyers beforehand. The independence and the differences in detail in the testimony to the resurrection – together with its basic unity and agreement – constitute a powerful argument for its sincerity and credibility.

Another point which needs stressing is that the evidence must be considered as a whole. It is comparatively easy to find an alternative explanation for one or another of the different strands which make up this testimony. But such explanations are valueless unless they fit the other strands in the testimony as well. A number of different theories, each of which might conceivably be applicable to part of the evidence but which do not themselves cohere into an intelligible pattern, can provide no alternative to the one interpretation which fits the whole.

Lastly, it can be asserted with confidence that men and women disbelieve the Easter story not because of the evidence but in spite of it. It is not that they weigh the evidence with open minds, assess its relevance and cogency and finally decide that it is suspect or inadequate. Instead, they start with the *a priori* conviction that the resurrection of Christ would constitute such an incredible event that it could not be accepted or believed without scientific demonstration of an

---

[4] Acts 2:24, NEB.
[5] Particularly if one regards the last few verses of Mark's Gospel as uncanonical.

irrefutable nature. But it is idle to demand proof of this sort
for any event in history. Historical evidence, from its very
nature, can never amount to more than a very high degree of
probability. It is on such evidence that virtually all our
knowledge of the past depends. Speaking of what he terms the
'Grand Miracle' of the incarnation, C. S. Lewis writes: 'If
the thing happened, it was the central event in the history of
the Earth – the very thing that the whole story has been
about. Since it happened only once, it is by Hume's standards
infinitely improbable. But then the whole history of the
Earth has also happened only once; is it therefore incredible?
Hence the difficulty, which weighs upon Christian and atheist
alike, of estimating the probability of the Incarnation. It is
like asking whether the existence of nature herself is intrinsi-
cally probable. That is why it is easier to argue, on historical
grounds, that the Incarnation actually occurred than to show,
on philosophical grounds, the probability of its occurrence.'[6]
Our argument in this book is that the evidence for the historical basis of the Christian faith, for the essential validity
of the New Testament witness to the person and teaching of
Christ himself, for the fact and significance of his atoning
death, and for the historicity of the empty tomb and the
apostolic testimony to the resurrection, is such as to provide an
adequate foundation for the venture of faith.

People often talk as though faith were some special endow-
ment – whether to be prized above rubies or distrusted as a
dangerous delusion – vouchsafed to certain types of persons;
and that it has little or no connection with an intelligent
appraisal of facts. This is, in my view, a grave misconception.
Some people, no doubt, are more credulous than others, and
to them faith may seem to come more easily than to most of
us. But true faith must always have a firm basis in reason,
although it must also, by its very nature, go beyond mere
reason. In every department of life we act on certain logical
and reasonable assumptions, but without a full understanding
of all that lies behind them. We use electricity, for example,
because we know what it can provide in the way of light,
heat and sound, and we understand something of how it does
so; but we do not fully understand the nature of electricity

[6] *Miracles*, pp. 112f.

itself. To say that we would never switch on the light, the fire or the radio till we had attained this perfect understanding would be a sign of stupidity, not intelligence. It would certainly make life somewhat bleak!

I am convinced that, in much the same way, the foundations of the Christian faith are such that it is an act of intelligence, not credulity, to take the decisive – yet responsive – step of self-committal to the living Christ. In the final analysis this means a person-to-person relationship which involves an outreach of our whole personality and differs fundamentally from the pursuit of historical investigation or the exercise of logical deduction. But the intellectual and the experimental are not contradictory. On the contrary, they go hand in hand, and the second confirms the first.

It is the professed purpose of John's Gospel to bring men and women not only to intellectual belief in the deity of Christ but also to a vital experience of the new life he gives, for towards the end of the Gospel we read: 'Now Jesus did many other signs in the presence of the disciples, which are not written in this book; but these are written that you may believe that Jesus is the Christ, the Son of God, and that believing you may have life in his name.'[7] In the First Epistle of John we find this put in even more vivid terms: 'That which was from the beginning, which we have heard, which we have seen with our eyes, which we have looked upon and touched with our hands, concerning the word of life – the life was made manifest, and we saw it, and testify to it, and proclaim to you the eternal life which was with the Father and was made manifest to us . . . And this is the testimony, that God gave us eternal life, and this life is in his Son. He who has the Son has life; he who has not the Son of God has not life. I write this to you who believe in the name of the Son of God, that you may know that you have eternal life.'[8]

Looking back over the ground covered by these chapters as a whole it seems to me that the point from which we started – the unique nature of the Christian message as this is presented in the New Testament – is sufficiently apparent. All the other world religions (and a great deal that goes by the name of Christianity too) try to teach men how they can earn salvation;

[7] Jn. 20:30, 31.　　　　　　　[8] I Jn. 1:1, 2; 5:11–13.

how they can climb up to heaven, as it were, to discover God; how they can atone for their own past sins; or how they can make themselves one with a holy God. The ethical teaching they give, with this end in view, may be more or less satisfactory according to the religion concerned. But the point I want to emphasize is that the New Testament states, in the most unequivocal terms, that this simply cannot be done. Men can never earn salvation, whatever they do; they can never climb up to heaven, for the gulf is far too wide; they can never atone for past sin, for they cannot live without sin in the present or the future; and they can never make themselves one with a holy God. All this is quite beyond man's power; it cannot – and indeed *need* not – be done. For it is precisely here that the good news of the incredible love and initiative of God himself comes to meet us in our need. This is the wholly unique element in the gospel; for it tells us that what we could never do, God has done. We could not climb up to heaven to discover God, but God has come to us in the person of his Son to reveal himself in the only way we could begin to understand. We could never atone for sin, but God in Christ has dealt with the problem of sin, once for all, at the crucifixion. We could never make ourselves one with a holy God, but God in Christ offers to come into our lives and our hearts, if we invite him in as Saviour and Lord, and to share with us his own divine life. Nor is this mere wishful thinking; it is sober fact, to which I and many others can testify in our experience.

# INDEX OF AUTHORS